D0090861

viral parenting

A GUIDE TO SETTING BOUNDARIES, BUILDING TRUST, AND RAISING RESPONSIBLE KIDS IN AN ONLINE WORLD

MINDY MCKNIGHT

GRAND CENTRAL
PUBLISHING

NEW YORK   BOSTON

Grand Central Publishing
Hachette Book Group
1290 Avenue of the Americas, New York, NY 10104
grandcentralpublishing.com
twitter.com/grandcentralpub

First Edition: April 2019

Grand Central Publishing is a division of Hachette Book Group, Inc. The Grand Central Publishing name and logo is a trademark of Hachette Book Group, Inc.

The publisher is not responsible for websites (or their content) that are not owned by the publisher.

The Hachette Speakers Bureau provides a wide range of authors for speaking events. To find out more, go to www.hachettespeakersbureau.com or call (866) 376-6591.

Library of Congress Cataloging-in-Publication Data

Names: McKnight, Mindy, author.
Title: Viral parenting : a guide to setting boundaries, building trust, and raising responsible kids in an online world / Mindy McKnight.
Description: First edition. | New York, NY : Grand Central Life & Style, 2019.
Identifiers: LCCN 2018044407| ISBN 978-15387-6219-6 (hardcover) |
  ISBN 978-1-5491-4110-2 (audio download) | ISBN 978-1-5387-6218-9 (ebook)
Subjects: LCSH: Parenting. | Child rearing. | Internet—Social aspects. |
  Technological innovations—Social aspects.
Classification: LCC HQ769 .M2325 2019 | DDC 306.874—dc23
LC record available at https://lccn.loc.gov/2018044407

ISBNs: 978-1-5387-6219-6 (hardcover); 978-1-5387-6218-9 (ebook)

Printed in the United States of America

LSC-C

10 9 8 7 6 5 4 3 2 1

Contents

PART III

FRIENDSHIP AND COMMUNITY

Introduction

Parenting in the digital twenty-first century needs a new rulebook.

Remember when you could shut your doors and what happened in your house stayed within its walls? Or when the worst post-bedtime transgression was reading a book by flashlight under the covers? Nowadays, your little one doesn't have to leave the house in order to be sneaking out after curfew, with fingers flying over that tiny keyboard to keep Snapchat streaks going or texting their friends into the wee hours of the night. Or posting a picture of their new Stan Smiths on Instagram.

Your kids are the Digital Native Generation.

It used to be that we'd learn parenting skills from our parents, but now our kids are teaching *us* how to deal with technology, the Internet, and social media, not one of which existed in such complicated digital form when we were growing up. Say good-bye to the era of analog parenting relics, and hello to the digitally wired-from-birth kids who are instantly savvier about features on their smartphones than we'll ever be.

So, yes, the rules have changed, but to adapt, first you have to know what the rules *are*. How can you keep up with what your kids are doing when they download apps and get bored with them before you've even looked at them once?

It is time to be an online digital parent. Yes, it's different, but it doesn't have to be scary. In this book I want to teach you how to set basic ground rules that will work no matter what is happening in the digital world, because the only thing I know for sure is that technology will always be a step ahead of us. So, for a parent, what's more important than understanding which apps are most popular at the moment is knowing how to set ground rules with your kids for how they interact and present themselves online.

As one of YouTube's top moms, who also has children who are digital influencers, I know social media, and so do my kids. Thanks to our work experience, using the very same tools our kids use to connect with others; the age range of our six children (from seven to eighteen); and our own age as young parents, my husband and I are uniquely positioned to share what structure works best for children in that range. Born in 1974 and 1978, respectively, we're both essentially what you would call "Xennials"—the micro-generation born in the late '70s and early '80s. Because we work in a digital space, we age *down* with our technologies but age *up* in our parenting.

We're the last generation, in fact, that grew up with an analog childhood, but now have a completely digital adulthood. When the digital era took over, we were young enough to be able to adapt quickly and use the technology readily and efficiently. But *our* parents have little-to-zero reference today to help teach *us* how to parent and raise our children, the first fully Digital Native Generation. (Our nickname for our parents' generation is the "Barely There" Digital Generation!) We're all learning as we go, but we hope that by sharing the rules we've established for our six different, hilarious, wonderful, exasperating, determined, tech-savvy, and opinionated kids—rules that we've tested and know truly work—you'll be able to create your own digital rules for the unique needs of your family.

Xennials have become a bridge of sorts between the analog and the digital worlds. Because our parents couldn't teach us how to parent in a digital world, we are by default the new-rule creators and influencers. Our children will take how we've raised and parented them and continue that as the standard for their future families. It's really kind of thrilling to be living through this enormous shift in cultural norms, and to be able to create a whole new paradigm for our children.

Our aim is to cover all bases as we teach you how to master these new technologies and platforms and apply the new rules to your own family structure. By involving ourselves in our children's ever-evolving technological world, we can effectively help them avoid fallout not only in their own lives but also the lives of others.

Much of the time, keeping up with what the kids do online is *fun*, but the downside to this always-connected world is that it can also be draining and even destructive. You must acknowledge the cons (naïve sharing of personal information, pornography, cyberbullying, and lack of interpersonal communication skills at a glance) while encouraging the pros (educational resources, digital community building, and quickly being able to contribute donations, for example, to victims of natural disasters).

How can a parent navigate these waters and mitigate potential pitfalls while providing their children the best opportunities to succeed? You *can* try to control what your kids do and have access to in your home, but you *can't* control what they do and what they're exposed to when they're outside of it. It used to be easier to keep them in a bubble of protection from the wildness of the world. Now, with Twitter and Instagram, they can find out if there's been a terrorist attack in Paris, France, or Paris, Ohio, within just a few minutes after it happens. Sometimes they know before the mainstream media reports on it. Our children are instantly wired on a global scale, and we don't always have a buffer to discuss and control how we frame the global world for them.

Social media never turns off. It's a 24/7 time snatcher. You can't escape it. You have to know how to control it before it controls you—and your children.

HOW TO USE THIS BOOK

Not only is this book full of our tried-and-true rules, best tips, and time-saving hacks (especially for parents balancing full-time work with the demands of family life), but you'll learn how to connect with your kids using the coded language of technology—and it *is* actually another language. In addition, our incredibly tech-savvy children, some of whom have achieved worldwide fame with their own social media channels, are sharing the best of what they know, making this book amazingly helpful not just for you but for your tweens and teens who want to learn from their peers.

In Part I, "Life Through a Selfie Stick: How Technology Has Transformed Parenting," we'll take you from the analog century and land you safely in the digital century. You'll learn how to use all the most popular social media platforms, what you don't need, and how important etiquette is. You can see the family contracts we've created that all our children must sign and abide by. Most important, we'll discuss in depth the pros and cons of social media as it relates to family and discuss appropriate digital citizenship.

In Part II, "Family and Home Life," we'll show you how to apply the new rules for technology to all aspects of family life. Setting up specific structures will help you define your approach to parenthood and allow your children to thrive. Our rules and philosophy will guide you through all the common parenting issues, from picking your battles to homework to chores to friendships and downtime. I'll give you strategies for instilling respect, parenting on the same page, and managing rivalries.

Part III, "Friendship and Community," deals with the issues our children face as friends, and with the unfortunate reality of bullying, both online and off. It also deals with *you* as a parent, as a friend, as a member of your extended family, and as part of your community. Without loving and supportive shoulders to cry on, it would be infinitely harder to parent our children—in good times and in bad. I've made many online friends that I likely will never meet, but they have given me as much advice as they've asked for, and these positive relationships have changed my life. In addition, we are a faith-driven family, and contributing to our community is important to us. Giving back to those in need is one of the best ways to take children offline and help them become citizens of the world.

We hope this book will become an indispensable guide for all your parenting questions, no matter where you live, how digitally savvy you are, and even if you still think you're an analog relic!

McKnight Relic Moment: Shaun walks in one day after school and begins to talk to Brooklyn and Bailey about them posting about their baes online. He pronounced it "bye," as in good-*bye*, rather than "bay."

Mindy: "Girls, how do you use this new app called Keek?"

BB: "Mom, it's KIK. Like kick!"

See what I mean?

HOW THIS BOOK CAME TO BE

It all started with a basic ponytail.

As I stood in our small bathroom, doing my daughters' hair before they went off to school each day, I never dreamed that my talent for braiding would make me a top mom on YouTube.

I could never have predicted that my nine-year-old twins, Brooklyn and Bailey, or my six-year-old daughter, Kamri, would go on to create their own YouTube channels, that they would eventually have millions of subscribers of their own, or that my family would go on tours across America and other countries.

I couldn't have imagined that those same hair tutorials would be viewed over 1 *billion* times in nearly every country in the world.

And I never, ever would have believed that the millions of moms, dads, and even children who follow us would start to send me hundreds of questions every day. Not just about hair—but about anything and everything family- and parenting-related.

I grew up in suburban Salt Lake City, Utah, the fourth of five children in a quintessential American family. My parents would be the first to say that I was supercompetitive and overachieving. I always wanted to be a mom, and wrote a story in second grade stating that I would have triplet girls when I got older (looks like I'm still shy of that goal by one, although people call Kamri the "Lagging Triplet!"— which makes her roll her eyes and laugh!).

Shaun grew up in Shelley, Idaho, a small potato-farming community. We met and fell in love as undergrads at Brigham Young University, got married a year before Shaun graduated (we decided that we wanted to be young parents so that we could be young grandparents!), and I graduated with eighteen-month-old twin girls on my hips. We were dirt-poor, but we made it work, in large part because of our upbringings and because our Mormon faith was very important to us. Most of the families we grew up with had lots of children, and many also had parents who overachieved both at work and in the home. These moms and dads were role models for us from the start. I have to admit that I'm one of those people who like to be busy and who work better under pressure.

As more children came along, we discovered two things: We were a girl-producing machine, and I was blessed with kids who had massive amounts of hair at a young age. I'd always loved doing hair, but it became more and more fun to work with as the girls got older. Every morning, we'd crowd into our little bathroom, me still with my jammies on (as you know!), and we'd run through spelling words or just talk about school, their friends, or whatever was planned for that day. They enjoyed Hair Time with Mom as much as I enjoyed creating different looks. In fact, if they were ever naughty, all I had to say was "No

Hair Time for you tomorrow," and they'd instantly start behaving! It was the perfect way to start the day.

As my girls grew, the styles became more elaborate, and as a time saver, I started making little photo flip-books so my girls could pick and choose which hairstyle they wanted that day. People would constantly compliment the girls on their hair and ask me how to replicate the styles. This was fun until people started asking me to *undo* their hair so that I could show them how to do it…right there in the grocery store or mall! A blog, I thought, would make it much easier to share my hobby and keep an online hair journal of sorts for the kids to reference when they were older. In 2008, I decided to start a blog to showcase the step-by-step photos I used to style my girls' hair, purely as a hobby.

In one of my smarter moves, I talked to a friend who worked as a website engineer and SEO expert, a professional in building and ranking websites in major search engines like Google. He said that, if we were serious, we needed a name with the right highly searched keywords in it. Thanks to his research, CuteGirlsHairstyles.com was born.

At first, the blog was basic—just photos and captions. I soon realized that some mommy bloggers were actually making money from their blogs, and I asked Shaun if we should put some ads up. He was dumbfounded. "Why would we do *that*?" he asked. "The only people looking at this are our friends and family. It would be really lame for them to have to look at ads on your blog when all they wanted was a hairstyle." I shrugged and tried to put some ads up anyway, but inadvertently implemented them wrong. This bugged my very computer-literate hubby so much that he went in and fixed it, and that was the beginning of Shaun's involvement in my online work.

The first month of monetizing the blog brought in a whopping $7. We were thrilled that this was enough money for an essentially "free" date-night burrito! Slowly, though, spread by word-of-mouth recommendations, my blog became more and more popular, and it soon earned several hundred dollars every month. (There was no better billboard for my hairstyles than having a little girl wear them to school and at church!) I was proud of my contribution to our family finances and happy that I could now afford to buy myself or the kids a new pair of jeans once in a while without feeling so pressed by our budget.

About six months later, I created a hairstyle that just wouldn't translate in photographs. Shaun had the brilliant idea of using his brand-new Flip Video camera (*remember them?*) to film me in the bathroom with the girls, and then uploading the video directly to YouTube so we could embed the video HTML code on our blog. I was shocked when YouTube got in touch with us a few months later and asked if we'd like to join the YouTube Partner Program. We were so clueless that Shaun had to do some research online to verify that it was a legitimate request and not a phishing scam. We signed on, quickly started earning, and realized that there was money to be made on YouTube, after all.

As the videos took off and our viewership rapidly increased, we soon realized that one of the reasons for our success was that styling hair is free, and it's a universal form of communication that transcends all spoken or written language. Because our followers didn't need to understand English to be able to follow what I was doing, our website quickly developed an international viewer base.

We had another surprise when, in May 2011, YouTube added us to its On the Rise competition where fans vote for one of four small up-and-coming channels. Whichever channel gets the most votes receives a channel feature on YouTube's home page for a full day. We did so well that we won by a larger margin than any previous winner. Little girls talked about how they'd voted on every single computer in the Apple store or the school computer lab because they loved us so much! We were thrilled when we won, and we gained approximately fifteen thousand new subscribers in the twenty-four hours that we were on YouTube's home page, an increase of 21 percent. That's when we realized we could potentially turn my little hobby into a truly viable and long-lasting career.

I was equally astonished that so many people were fascinated by our family "behind the braids" videos. At first, they asked me about the kids: where they got their clothes, their hobbies, schoolwork, how I managed to get everything done, house rules, chores, how I coped with six young children, if I had paid help, and more. Very soon, those questions became more moving and complicated: How does a parent raise good kids? How do you keep them grounded? What are your secrets?

I soon realized that, as our popularity grew, our followers' children were growing up with *our* children, which made moms feel comfortable with me. They saw me as someone also struggling to balance a life full of kids, my now full-time job, education, and after-school activities and to maintain a healthy relationship with my wonderful husband.

Me doing hair in my jammies in front of the bathroom mirror was a large part of our appeal—millions of other moms did the same thing, too. It was relatable. We used a battered old camping light with tin foil around it to add and reflect extra lighting in the beginning. No tripods or microphones, and no editing at all. Those early hairstyle videos were done in *one* take, with Shaun standing behind me with his Flip camera. I look back at them now and see how unprofessional and hokey they were! But that was very much what our followers loved and remains part of our story and culture today. I rarely showed my face, and we avoided showing the kids' faces most of the time, too. We called the kids CGH1 and CGH2, etc., for many years because we were very concerned about safety issues online. Eventually, as our viewership grew, we realized the lighting needed to be better in order to showcase the hairstyling details, so we fashioned a spare bedroom into a comfortable set and rigged up higher-quality but affordable lighting.

As we became more comfortable with filming, Brooklyn and Bailey decided that they wanted to be more than just hair models—they wanted to talk about what they liked to do, eat, and wear. When they turned thirteen, we allowed them to make their own YouTube channel as a place where our family could post vlogs, fashion videos, cooking tutorials, and anything else that didn't relate to hair. (Viewers had been asking for content like this from us, but it just didn't seem to fit on a hairstyle channel.) Today, it's still a very demanding job for the girls.

Around the same time, a network on YouTube asked me to anchor an online series for moms. I filmed fifty-two five-minute parenting advice videos, and they did so well that it deepened my previous desire to share similar parenting-oriented content on my own channel. YouTube's demographic at the time was skewed quite young—mostly high school and college-age students—and as a result, Shaun and I were practically considered "online" grandparents! I know we wanted to be young parents, but I didn't realize I would be a young "online grandparent" quite so fast! ☺ Luckily for us, that also meant that there were few other options available for those who wanted to view parenting-oriented videos on YouTube.

Just like the parents of newborns, digital content creators were feeling their way along, and everyone—YouTube personalities, advertisers, and even YouTube itself—was thrilled when this type of media turned into such a juggernaut. Our channel was never sexy or flashy; it was about hairstyling, learning a new skill, being a mom, and parenting. It was extremely gratifying to realize that my decision to add parenting alongside our hairstyle channel had been the right call.

Today, of course, YouTube offers much more family content. The platform has grown up and recognized the appeal of family entertainment—videos that parents watch with their kids. Over the years, our channel has also evolved a little bit as well. We've pulled the family content forward even more by launching *Behind the Braids*, a vlog series that showcases our family in everyday situations. Our hair content remains popular as a useful evergreen reference, but creating more family-oriented content keeps us relevant.

We are the Tortoise in this story, not the Hare. It's taken YouTube over a *decade* to figure out what kind of content it is looking to promote and which content brings in the highest ad revenue, and viewer preferences have taken nearly as long to fully develop. Those preferences will most definitely shift, which is why being able to adapt is essential. Many of our earliest subscribers still follow me today. Back then, our channel catered to moms with young children; now, those little kids have become tweens or teens who want to do their own hair. Some subscribers were teenagers when we started and are now young moms with their own children. Thinking about that kind of makes me feel old in a funny way, but I'm incredibly delighted to be growing with our audience!

It also made me realize that being a mom was a lot like making my hair how-to's. Sometimes there were literally hours and hours of work and preparation for a one-minute shot. Viewers only saw the final version—not the research and the practice (often on my long-hair mannequin heads, Anna and Hannah, who still scare the pants off me when I walk into the bathroom and forget they're there!) and all the mistakes I made along the way. But the more I did it, the better my handiwork looked and the more quickly I figured things out.

To this day, I couldn't tell you how I came up with all my hairstyling ideas and skills. Some came easy as I had been doing them for years; others took a ton of work. I didn't always create the hairstyles myself, rather sometimes relying on my hair-dar (the ability to see great hairstyles everywhere you go and add your own flair), and I never had any professional training. I simply found out that I was really good at it. I also learned that I have an innate ability to see an image or a video of a hairstyle, figure out how it was prepared, break that process down into small segments, eliminate any unnecessary steps, and teach it to other people with easy-to-follow efficiency.

Likewise, I learned to approach each parenting problem as a puzzle. I dismantle, dissect, and de-clutter the many minuscule pieces and parts of the issue and share my new understanding in small, incremental pieces that make sense to other people. I try to give my followers easy, usable solutions to their hairstyling problems, and I try to give people easy, usable solutions to their parenting problems, too. Sometimes it's not even about solving the problem for them, but rather just giving them enough other ideas or thoughts to help them figure out the solution themselves.

Shaun and I realized that having a successful family is somewhat similar to running a successful workplace, but with a lot more love. Both require strategy, budgets, planning ahead, accountability, good corporate culture, having a Plan B and a Plan C in case Plan A doesn't work—and the creativity to improve and adapt as needed. As our family grew, we couldn't just plan ahead. We had to see each of our children for who they truly were so we could best meet their needs. Every day, I get them off to school, work full-time, get the house cleaned, shop for and cook good meals, make sure the kids get home, shuttle them to sports and music lessons, supervise homework, get them tucked in, and sometimes still have time to take a bath, make plans for the future, pay the bills, and say hello to Shaun (who is my equal partner in all this)!

Every mom knows how overwhelming parenting can be when a thousand things are pulling you in every direction, and how easy it is to get bogged down in how to do it all at the same time. I often joke that we're almost like the Von Trapp family from *The Sound of Music*: A whistle is blown, and everyone marches down the steps and obediently lines up. Okay, I *am* kidding, because, like every family, we also have emotions running high, temper tantrums, and squabbles all the time, but we also have a very specific routine. For our household to run smoothly, we've had to develop rules and a system that works for us.

We've made thousands of mistakes in the course of getting our family here, but we've learned a *lot* along the way. Being a full-time mom and a full-time digital media expert at the same time hasn't been easy. We're not perfect, but we try!

In fact, even though my family is now in the public eye, I still consider myself your typical everyday mom. Though it's hard for me to think of myself as unique, I know I've created something original that resonates strongly with millions of girls and their moms and helps those families to improve, too. I am very lucky to have been raised with such a strong sense of family, a sturdy work ethic, and faith, all of which have shown me the importance of rules, boundaries, and structure. I strive to do my work with integrity and to raise my children with loving guidance. At the end of the day, that is what we all want as parents—to raise compassionate, kind, thriving children who can figure out their purpose and find the happiness they deserve.

MEET THE MCKNIGHT CHILDREN

Brooklyn and Bailey

Our oldest kids, the twins, were born on New Year's Eve in 1999—yes, the waning hours of the second millennium.

What a way to ring in the New Year! From birth, they charmed every person they met with their bubbly personalities and penchant for getting people to smile. I guess you could say they are contagiously fun girls who love to sing, perform, and meet their viewers. I learned quickly with two babies that it takes a village to raise children. Family, friends, and sometimes even perfect strangers were helpers and givers of kindness when I needed extra arms to carry, bounce, feed, or otherwise learn how to become a new mom to two babies. Now, if we can just get them to keep their room clean!

Kamri

Born in 2002, Kamri is the girl who inspires us by choosing soccer and basketball instead of traditional girly stuff. She knows the most arcane facts about the most unusual topics, and wears me down with her incessant begging for the latest Twitter trend she saw that day. The twins certainly know how to steal a room, but when Kamri walks in, people are struck not just by her beauty but also by her quiet dignity. You don't even have to hear her speak to be drawn to her.

Rylan

Born in 2005, Rylan also started out as a twin, but we lost her sibling during pregnancy. She has more personality than all our other children combined, and an especially wonderful sense of humor. I also call Rylan my little "button pusher"— out of all my kids, she's the most likely to have the sibling sitting next to her in tears. Like her older sisters, she has an amazing voice and is the one most likely to be heard belting out Taylor Swift songs when she's in the shower. She's creative and talented and sees life as one giant game.

Daxton

Our only son and first adopted child was born in 2008. We were there for his delivery, and I held his mother's leg while she pushed him out! It was a truly beautiful experience when, after I cut the cord that bound him to his first mother, the doctor placed him into my waiting arms as his second mother. We tell him all the time that he is so special that he was blessed with two mommies that love him. Dax has been diagnosed with a hyposensitivity disorder, all three subtypes of ADHD, and level 1 autism. He sometimes struggles with simple things, especially those that require fine motor skills or social skills. Tasks like tying his shoes, making friends, and handwriting are difficult for him, but he's academically brilliant. We quickly learned that sports weren't his thing, but thankfully, he's discovered passions for coding and engineering. At any given time, you can find him writing simple apps, programming drones, or creating webpages and avatars. We've struggled and grown the most as parents because of Daxton, and wouldn't have it any other way.

Paisley

Our youngest daughter and second adopted child was born in 2011. Shaun and I missed her emergency early delivery because we lived on the other side of the country, but we hopped on a red-eye flight and met her ten hours later. She's a ray of sunshine and oozes love, always ready for a snuggle or a hug. Born with three unexpected heart conditions, she has defied the odds and lives a normal, healthy life. Her only limitation is that she can't ever scuba dive. I entered the world of natural hair care with Paisley and Dax and have learned so much from having a totally different type of hair in the house. The one most likely to sneak food (and hide the wrappers all over the house), Paisley's the perfect little caboose to our family.

PART I

Life Through a Selfie Stick: How Technology Has Transformed Parenting

Chapter 1

That Was Then, This Is Now

I grew up in suburban Salt Lake City, Utah, the fourth of five children. We'd come home from school, plunk down our backpacks, watch the one cartoon that was on TV, eat a snack, and run outside to play until it got dark. All the kids in the neighborhood knew each other, and the parenting was almost communal. We'd play at one house until the parents got sick of us and kicked us out, then we'd move to the next yard like a little wolf pack until, eventually, one of the parents would feed us a peanut butter and jelly sandwich on mushy white bread or some mac and cheese. Then my dad would get "done" with work and whistle for us to come home, and off we'd run to get cleaned up for dinner.

Our world was so small back then, but it felt big enough.

Nowadays, of course, it's nearly impossible to imagine our kids having the same freedom of movement—just as it's almost impossible for our kids to believe what my childhood was like. Yes, it's always reassuring to know that I can keep tabs on my kids wherever they are—and be glad that they can always reach me instantly in case of any problems—but I often think about how this ease of communication we now take for granted has affected me and every other mom I know. I mean, my parents *knew* they couldn't find us in a nanosecond when we were playing with our friends. They had a pretty good idea of where we might be, but that was about it. Did they fret? No, because they had no choice. That's just the way it was. No one *expected* to be tracked. Now we panic or veer into near-paranoia if the kids forget their cell phones one day or if someone loses the signal, despite the fact that crime statistics are lower than they were when Shaun and I were growing up, and it is extremely unlikely that anything would happen to our kids if we aren't able to find them for an hour or two!

The digital age has totally shifted not just how we parent, but everything we deal with on a daily basis. When Shaun and I got married in 1998 and started our family, the technology that allowed us to become YouTubers and digital influencers literally didn't exist. We have had to think outside the box, making the rules up as we go, as we built our business from the ground floor.

When I first started blogging, I never dreamed that my hobby would become not just a career, but eventually a family brand. I don't think any of us could have foreseen what the Internet and social media have morphed into…the good (thousands of ideas, worldwide community, and information at your fingertips) and the bad (invasions of privacy, cyberbullying, and fraud). You can share family photos with cousins on the other side of the world, or post a totally innocuous comment that can be misinterpreted and cause all sorts of hurt feelings when none were intended!

When I started thinking about the best way to show you just how much has changed from analog to digital, I found myself doing this side-by-side comparison of a parenting day from thirty years ago vs. a parenting day now. I was amazed to see how many things we take for granted and use or do every day that have completely changed from when we were young children. Many of these changes have made life so much easier and better, while others may leave you wishing for simpler days. It's kind of stunning how long this list is!

THE ANALOG VS. DIGITAL LIST

It's amazing how so much of what we used is now considered a relic that leaves our kids rolling their eyes! The digital shift is life as our kids have always known it and will continue to know it—this is what their world looks like to them every day, and they can't imagine it any other way.

Alarm Clock

Analog: Wind it up and hope it goes off, or plug in a bulky block with glowing red-green numbers that annoys you in your dark room.

Digital: Annoying beep on your cell phone with a snooze button that's way too easy to use. For an extra jolt, if a stranger has your "morning alarm" as his/her ring tone on their own phone, and someone calls them, your heart skips a beat in a conditioned response and you drop into an instant cold sweat before realizing it isn't actually your alarm!

Appointment Reminders

Analog: A postcard in the mail as a reminder, a quick phone call reminder, or a handwritten appointment card. Good luck keeping track of that.

Digital: Add the appointment directly to your smartphone calendar with the push of a button, complete customizable reminder notifications. Text reminders sent from your doctors and dentists.

Blackboards

Analog: Chalk and erasers on the blackboard, those horrible overhead projectors, or if you were lucky, a whiteboard with dry-erase markers.

Digital: SMART Boards. Teachers mirror their laptops direct to the screen, navigating with a fingertip to Google, homework papers, or other needed teaching materials such as YouTube videos. They can even save what they draw on the SMART Boards for future lessons.

Card Games

Analog: Sitting with your friends and a deck of cards, playing UNO, slap jack, or any other game where you almost always had the full deck.

Digital: Online and app-based games, where you play on your smartphone to answer questions in real time or play your hands. (You can learn how to play games like hearts or poker online, playing against the computer if you are playing alone, or you can play with your friends. The apps can then display the answers or hands on the TV screen. It's so sophisticated that up to a hundred people can play at a time!)

Cars

Analog: Using a key to lock the doors and start the car, analog dials, running down the battery if you forgot to turn off the lights, and having to judge the distance behind and around the car before you moved. And of course, needing a good road atlas for long trips that you'd begin with only the vaguest sense of when you would arrive.

Digital: Keyless locks, integrated GPS, lights that turn themselves on and off, doors that open themselves, heated seats, so many digital features you never use them, etc. You can now start your car remotely, and adjust the temperature before leaving your house. TV entertainment for children is a *must* with headphones, and USB chargers in multiple locations. You can even use Bluetooth to connect your phone and listen to Spotify or a great podcast when you're stuck in traffic. With innovations from Tesla, cars are doing what we all dreamed of in the analog days…they can drive themselves!

Coffee

Analog: Folgers or Maxwell House from the grocery store, or (horrors!) family-size instant powder and gross coffee filters.

Digital: Home espresso machines so complicated it takes an engineering degree to figure out how to use them, so you go to Starbucks instead and pay with an app, or use a single-serve Keurig machine with any number of flavors.

Coloring Books

Analog: Using crayons or colored pencils on newsprint paper in thin books that tore easily.

Digital: Swipe your finger to pick a variety of colors, and color your online masterpieces.

Computers and Word Processors

Analog: Manual typewriters, electric typewriters (and the wonder of correction tape), word processors with floppy discs, bulky desktop computers with barely any memory, and dot-matrix printers that always jammed and gave you printouts that were impossible to read.

Digital: Lightweight, slim laptops with terabytes of memory, or iPads, and now even the Apple Watch! Even printers are digital, wireless, and some can fit in your shirt pocket.

Design Tips

Analog: Reading *Better Homes and Gardens* magazines at the library or watching Martha Stewart on TV.

Digital: Pinterest, Instagram, or YouTube DIY tutorials.

Disputes (Trivial)

Analog: Asking around to get a group consensus, looking up information in reference books, or agreeing to disagree with no conclusive resolution about who is right about a piece of information.

Digital: Asking Siri, Alexa, or your favorite browser for an answer, which is delivered in under twenty seconds, depending on how well you searched.

Getting Paid

Analog: Receiving a mailed check, waiting in line to hand it to a teller to deposit, and then waiting several days for it to clear.

Digital: Direct deposit, PayPal, Venmo, or if you're paid with a check, you can simply take a photo on your phone and send it directly to your bank for instant deposit.

Getting to School

Analog: Waiting on the corner in the freezing rain for the school bus to show up.

Digital: Checking your school district's school bus tracking app so your kids can leave the house right before it shows up.

Health

Analog: Mom diagnosis, or you finally go to the doctor. If you're a certain age, you may even remember a doctor who made house calls!

Digital: Tele-medicine with a doctor online. Online websites that help diagnose what is wrong (and convince you that your symptoms automatically mean you have a horrible ailment). You can even buy your prescription glasses online.

Homework

Analog: Writing it all down in pen or pencil in notebooks, storing them in folders or Trapper Keepers, or filling in handouts from teachers to be returned the next day.

Digital: Google Classroom—just type it up online and submit the homework to the teacher right there. Kids can also upload project files, and direct-message the teacher or classmates. Grades are also given online.

Life Skills

Analog: Learn only the things your parents, relatives, or close friends also know how to do.

Digital: Online tutorials that can teach a soccer mom how to rewire her home or a dad how to French-braid his daughter's hair.

Music

Analog: AM radio, FM radio, largely determined by which DJs and show hosts you knew shared your tastes. LPs on the record player, 8-tracks, cassettes, CDs, a Walkman or boombox (practically as large as your child). Headphones large enough to give you a headache and that had to be connected via a short wire.

Digital: Omnipresent streaming of unlimited music, from all genres, on your cell phone. Earphones that are wireless, noise-canceling, or nearly impossible-to-see earbuds.

News Events

Analog: The morning and evening newspapers delivered to your door, covering yesterday's news, or a 6 p.m. newscast.

Digital: Alerts on your cell phone, breaking news within seconds of it happening via social media. And because so many more people are able to deliver the news—from your friends to bloggers to commentators—there are so many more voices talking to us about what's happening in the world than there used to be!

Photography

Analog: A camera with film that had to be developed, Polaroids for instant gratification, developing the film and discovering that only seventeen of your thirty-two exposures were any good, and impossible-to-take selfies.

Digital: Digital cameras with instant results, screens that show you exactly what the photo will look like, photo-editing apps that make any photo look like it was professionally taken, majority of photos taken are "selfies."

Recording Devices

Analog: Mini or full-size tape recorders with cassettes. I remember going to school plays or recitals where every single dad was sitting or crouching at the end of the stage with a giant camera on his shoulder, taping it all for posterity. **Digital:** Digital recorders that are so small, they are often impossible to see, some with voice dictation that automatically uploads voice files to your computer and translates them into multiple languages in an instant.

Shopping

Analog: Going to the mall or department stores like Macy's, Sears, or Kmart with a finite amount of cash. **Digital:** Using a stylist to send you digital boards, online shopping, Amazon, Etsy, or apps to post pictures of items you've seen and others tell you where to buy. Shopping on credit with no real sense of a limit. Paying by simply holding your phone up to a sensor. Free shipping and free returns from smart merchants all around the world.

Studying

Analog: Going to the library, riffling through the card catalog using the Dewey Decimal System, finding the books, sitting at a table, and taking notes till your hand was about to fall off. If you were lucky, your library had a copy machine. **Digital:** Hitting the Google button and finding what you need instantly, and bookmarking for future use.

Telephones—at Home

Analog: Landlines with phone jacks and cords that always got tangled, zero to little privacy, and a busy signal if the person you were calling was talking to someone else. Oh, the joys when Call Waiting and Caller ID were invented!

Digital: Cell phones that basically run your life 24/7, and double as an entertainment device and a supercomputer in your pocket.

Telephones—Outside

Analog: Pay phones on the corner that were usually broken, or you had to wait in line behind someone who just wouldn't stop yakking. You had to carry around a quarter at all times in case you had to make a call. Calling long distance cost a lot of money. Remember calling collect?

Digital: Cell phones with unlimited minutes, to anywhere in the world for the same monthly price. Most commercial places have community charging stations where you can charge your device.

Television

Analog: Only three to four channels, a large and squatty box, and you actually had to get up off the couch and change the channel yourself or use a basic remote. Many had bunny-ear antennae, which you often had to adjust to get a better signal.

Digital: Flat screens with vibrant color, apps that act as universal remotes, multiple channel watching at the same time, or use to connect to your favorite streaming services. Watch in HD or in 3-D.

Watching Movies

Analog: Dad brings home one VHS tape rented from a local store or from Blockbuster, and slips it into the VCR player.

Digital: Binge-watching your favorite flicks on YouTube or Netflix, or buying them on iTunes, streamed instantly 24/7, on any device, and having the kids squabble over who gets to watch what, when!

I've spent a lot of time discussing these topics with people all over the world and with parents from all backgrounds. Despite differences based on culture and location, I find that most parents currently live in one of two different groups. Both are good parents trying to sort out how to navigate this digital space. Both want the best for their children. And both are doing some things right and some things wrong.

Group 1 is our "Head in the Sand" parents. The myth has it that when an ostrich gets scared, rather then having a typical fight-or-flight response, the ostrich will simply stand in the same spot and bury its head in the ground. Even if true, this obviously wouldn't really help the ostrich as it would still be in imminent danger, but it wouldn't see the danger anymore so it might feel better for a few seconds. I feel like there are a lot of parents doing this very thing right now. They don't understand social media, and because they don't, it scares them. They sit in church or watch the news or visit with other parents and hear horror stories about kids that use social media to plot murders, watch pornography, find drugs, or do any number of other things they don't want their kids involved with. Since they have no experience in parenting digital native children and because they were raised in an analog world, they panic. Freeze up. Stick their heads in the sand, hoping that when they pull their heads back out, the digital space will not only have gone away but will have been replaced with the much more comfortable analog space they grew up with and know how to manage.

They often refuse their children digital experiences by not allowing or very strictly limiting cell phones, the Internet, or any type of tablet. Sometimes even going as far as removing their children from schools, where other children have digital devices. They would prefer their children to be raised in their well-worn analog world and they try to re-create that existence. The problem with this group is that by keeping their kids in this analog bubble, they are failing to teach them how to navigate the digital waters, with the language and understanding needed when they do, in fact, go digital. If you stop to think about how many touch points you have in one day that are digital, it's easy to realize digital isn't going away. But not giving kids the skills when they are younger and you can control and help navigate their experiences can, in fact, hurt them in the long run.

Group 2 is our "total freedom" parenting group. These parents are savvy enough to know that digital is here to stay. They like being their child's friend and don't know how to make digital rules or simply don't want to. They also want their kids to be socially accepted so they get their children the most current devices, phones, and computers, and allow their children complete freedom on digital platforms. Sometimes they are just too exhausted with trying to keep up with digital changes so they just give up. They didn't have all the social media as analog children and believe that, since they don't currently use their own devices in terrible ways, neither do their children. This can lead to them giving their children as young as seven or eight a cell phone because it makes life more convenient. They don't fully understand the world their children live in and the possible pitfalls facing digital native children. They may even naïvely believe that if something truly terrible were happening, their children would alert them. The problem with this group is that the parents' lack of awareness and understanding often gives kids too much freedom. Not setting limits or staying aware of their child's digital space can be dangerous and potentially damaging, especially if this child has been exposed to or has experienced situations they were unaware of.

Neither group is wrong or bad. But they are very different. My goal is to create Group 3: a parenting group where parents realize the beauty and power of social media, but also realize that it can be a minefield for kids to navigate. A group of parents who are empowered in their knowledge of how social media platforms work, and having loving, open conversations with their kids about what they are experiencing and seeing online. A group of parents who are actively involved online alongside their children, teaching them social etiquette online as well as how to create positivity in online spaces.

The more digital you become as parents, the better guides you will be for your kids as they navigate the awesome, amazing experiences available to all in the digital world. Shaun and I soon realized we needed to be proactive and create a set of rules so we could harness the amazing power of the digital world and make it as safe as possible for our children, and for our own use, too. What you'll find in the next few chapters is our family's guidelines and rules that we've developed and refined over the years. Think of them as a template for creating your own family rules that feel right for you—as thought starters so you can decide what will and won't work within your own home. You might think at first that some of these rules are too strict (and decide never to give your kids a cell phone!), or you might think they're not strict enough (and decide to take the cell phones away!). What I hope is that you'll easily find the middle ground, a place where your kids will learn the best of how to be digital and responsible yet still have touch points to wisdom and the analog world.

So let's take a deep look at how the digital world shapes how we communicate and share information.

Chapter 2

What Is This New Digital Space and Why Do We Need It?

KNOW YOUR INTERNET!

Shaun: "There are three mathematical formulas ruling the world right now: the algorithms run by Google/YouTube, Twitter, and Facebook. What does this mean? Well, AI is basically learning its way through how to categorize and rank everything discoverable online, and displaying the top results based upon a user's interests within an entity-established set of boundaries. You may set initial limits by what you search, but how the AI does what it does is fully out of your control. Eventually the AI knows so much about you, the ads served are for products you would likely buy, but you have not searched for them previously. Essentially, these algorithms can guess more accurately what you are looking for than you can yourself. What's scary about these algorithms and this AI is that this behind-the-scenes power is something that will never be shared openly with you. Also, in a way, AI takes away your own right to choose what you see organically, or any alternative view, because a machine is selecting your top options for you.

"It wouldn't be unfathomable in the future for a machine to eventually give us no other choice than the one it selects for us. We would simply coast through life taking the only available step placed right in front of us. This is a very scary thought. We've historically been afraid of human dictators who make choices for populations, but we should be equally as concerned with AI for the same reasons.

"Why am I starting this chapter with this information? Because everything you do online is being tracked. I am not talking about the government, as many would assume. Tracking is being done so that merchants can place targeted ads on Google, YouTube, Facebook, or other platforms in the hopes of getting a sale. That's normal business today, and the more you pay attention to what's happening on the screen, the more you're going to notice it. It might be annoying or even a bit creepy when you search for a pair of snow boots on Amazon, shut down for the night, and then see a bunch of snow boot ads in the morning, no matter what site you visit!

"This is AI at work, behind the scenes.

"Two things worry me about the future. One is that alternate reality will become more desirable than our real-life physical reality—that everything will be so virtually perfect that a faux concert will literally make you feel as if you're in the front row. We're already seeing hints of this if you go to a real concert and realize that people in the audience are so busy recording it on their cell phones that they're not paying attention to the music! The other is that information is going to be served to us by a machine that's trying to *predict* what we want, instead of what we *do* want. But the machine can't learn what you're thinking; it can only gauge future interests based upon your past actions. So someone who knows how to control algorithms could deliberately serve you very specific information that you're not even aware of. It's bad enough for a news station to have an agenda, as they should be making a clear distinction between reporting the factual news and their commentary/political slant, and a different thing for a service, like Google or Facebook, that's supposed to be impartial, to steer information on a pendulum to everybody.

"The point I'm getting to—and why this information is so crucial—is that in our digital age, there's no such thing as neutrality. You'll always have to be aware that what you're seeing has some kind of bias. It's absolutely crucial to teach your children how to be critical thinkers, online and off, so they can assess what's biased or not and make informed decisions using the most reliable sources.

"And, of course, becoming critical thinkers is one of the best things possible for children, as it will help them with all their life decisions, both analog and digital. Critical thinking looks very different at different ages. At age six, critical thinking questions about social media would likely include lessons such as how did that make me feel? Does this make me feel sad or happy?

"When I was working towards the carpentry merit badge in Boy Scouts, my scoutmaster told us, 'Measure twice, cut once.' In other words, be sure you've got it right before you make that cut and then realize you've wasted the whole expensive piece of wood and your time because you weren't careful enough.

"That principle of 'Think twice, post once' is even more essential in social media today because social media is like *cut, cut, cut*. Kids often don't think before they post, so as a parent, you have to tell them, think twice, edit twice, and *then* post once. You have to apply the principles of critical thinking to every aspect of digital life. Control it so it doesn't control you. (And as you'll see in this chapter, it's really not difficult at all to gain this control!)

"It's so important to drill 'Think twice, post once' into your kids so they always, *always* ask themselves if-then scenarios, or what we in business call decision-tree analysis. As in, 'If I post this, what are the potential outcomes?' I know there will be positive comments and negative comments. What will the scope of the negative comments be? Will the positive outweigh it? Are the people who'll see my post going to be left better off than before I posted it? Am I doing this because I'm in a bad mood or what I read left me so angry I felt I had to share it?

"All these decisions are made very quickly, especially when kids are texting, but even young children who just got their first phone can understand this rule. But you have to teach it to them, set explicit boundaries, and monitor their use."

SHAUN, ON SETTING GROUND RULES

How do you talk to your kids about critical thinking, and how do you edit these conversations depending on the age of your children and your family's life experiences? What kinds of critical thinking could we all be doing to have a better perspective on what we see happening online? These are basic questions or tests that Mindy and I use so our kids can judge what's real vs. what's fake, and are able to perceive hidden agendas, such as sponsored content that is actually just an ad for a new toy or gadget.

One thing I learned from a wonderful book called *Parenting with Love and Logic* was that setting the rules when kids are little means the price tags for mistakes are also little. If the kids are teens, setting new rules should become the norm (just brace yourself for a bit of grumbling!). We live in a digital world and it is never going back to analog, so the sooner everyone learns the digital language and the rules of its use, the easier it is to process.

Our kids quickly become so fluent in the digital language that we as parents are often still learning, but on the other hand, *we* have the analog knowledge of the adult world and all its foibles that they do not. It's time to share the digital and analog know-how in an age-appropriate way, so everyone can reap the benefits online and off.

YES, THE INTERNET IS FOREVER

Tweens and teens do remember that anything they post online can be captured with a screenshot and passed around, but it's hard for them to grasp the notion that college recruiters or future employers might look at their youthful exuberance and judge it a tad more harshly than their peers! Knowing that the Internet is forever isn't the same as *believing* it. It's not an easy idea to grasp at a young age, and often, it takes a tangible consequence or a touch point to someone else feeling a tangible consequence for this notion to become vivid reality.

Kids think in the present. That's what makes them kids, and so much fun to be around. For a thirteen-year-old, college is five or six years away, which is eons in Teen Time. Full-time employment is too far off to even contemplate!

Something we've learned from being YouTubers is that it's not even just what you post, it's how you act in public that can be forever, too—because everyone's a paparazzi, armed with a cell phone camera and a share button. For example, last year at VidCon, a video-centered convention for YouTubers and other digital influencers, a very well-known YouTube personality didn't have the right pass to get into the venue, and because he was young and frustrated, he pulled a "Don't you know who I am?" routine to the security guard, who clearly *didn't* know who he was. This was a video convention, remember, so what do you think every teenager did? They pulled out their phones and recorded the YouTuber's tantrum. This poor guy got a bad rap for his behavior—not because he posted it online, but because he had a meltdown in a public area. He forgot that people were always watching him in the heat of the moment.

That was an extremely potent lesson for all our kids. Now, regardless of whether your kids have a big following online or no social media accounts at all, it's a good idea for them to behave in a way that they'd be okay having broadcast across YouTube. As a parent, you can put filters on your kids' social media accounts so that curse words or your address can be filtered out and your kids won't even notice. But when you send your kids out the door, there is no physical filter from the world. They need to be prepared. It's up to you to teach them that anything they say or do can be recorded for posterity, whether it's something that portrays them in a good light or a bad light. Not to make them paranoid—just to make them *aware.* The best way to get this message across is to teach your children good manners, to be kind, and to treat others with respect.

Easier said than done, since even the most well-behaved and loving kids have days where they say and do things they regret or don't mean. That's life. We all mess up. It's the messes we make that teach us the most memorable lessons of what *not* to do!

For example, Brooklyn had her heart broken when she was unexpectedly dumped by her longtime boyfriend. I wondered that night if she would "angry" text him, but decided to wait and see what she would do. So I monitored her texts via her computer's iMessage app just in case I needed to intervene. Sure enough, within a few hours a couple of angry texts went out. I immediately went to her room and took her phone away. I knew at the time she was upset and this made her even more frustrated. But I also knew that she was going to continue to send texts, likely increasing in intensity. Brooklyn came back to me later the next day and thanked me for taking her phone away. She said, "It kept me from letting my emotions take control, and texting hurtful words because I hoped he would feel as much pain as I do." Her ex didn't deserve that, and it saved her from potential embarrassment as well. We also talked about what a screenshot of her hurtful texts could have meant for her brand. It was a valuable lesson and I'm glad I trusted my gut.

This is the kind of help that children need from parents, even if they don't realize it. My kids know that technology is a privilege in our house; as you'll see later in the book, everyone has to agree to a set of rules before they are allowed a phone, or laptop, or other device. Because those rules are established early on, I didn't have to get into a huge fight with my daughter about her privacy, or negotiate with her when she was already in a painfully emotional place about what behavior was or wasn't okay. You'll also see in subsequent chapters how to set up rules that make sense for your household so that you have a clear path forward in those heated moments.

NOTHING ONLINE IS PRIVATE

Further to the inescapable fact that the Internet is forever is the knowledge that nothing online should ever be thought of as truly and 100 percent completely private. This is an issue for both kids and their parents.

Because so much information can be shared so quickly, privacy issues have become blurred. It's really hard for kids to know what should remain private, such as information about family members with illnesses, or someone losing a job, or a friend who's depressed, or not. Kids aren't often able to keep secrets, even when they promise they will. When I was a kid, a private secret that somehow became public stayed contained in a very small arena. Now the whole world can know about it in a nanosecond with the press of a button.

Parents need to start considering privacy issues from the time their children are born. Your babies and small children are so adorable and photogenic, so of course you want to share photos and cute captions and all sorts of information. Once you do, however, those images and that information become public, and forever out of your control.

If you blog or post regularly on Facebook or Instagram, you can easily control who sees your postings with the different privacy settings. They are there for a reason, so use them! You can set up a Facebook page that is secret for trusted friends and family members only, and post whatever you like. Assuming, of course, that these people you trust will abide by your rules about not sharing—but most people are honorable when you ask them to be.

Set boundaries and rules for your own posting. Think twice, post once. If you have any doubts, don't post. If your kids are older, ask their permission first. If they say yes, great. If they said yes last year and now beg you to remove a story or photo, listen to them. It's *their* story, not yours.

SHARING VS. OVERSHARING, OR NOT EVERYONE NEEDS TO KNOW WHAT YOUR PIZZA LOOKS LIKE

When I was growing up, the thought that perfect strangers would be interested in the meals my family ate or what I wore to school was incomprehensible. Even today, I would never dream of sharing a selfie of everything I do, because I certainly don't think it's important enough to share!

Our kids think otherwise. The fact that the word "selfie" even exists just about says it all, right? Kids use selfies and other pictures to journal their day-to-day activities in real time for anyone to see.

I think it's human nature to share insights and things you've learned with people you trust and love. It always has been. You move to a new area and meet a new friend, and you're going to go on a date night with your husband or significant other, and the first thing you ask your new friend is, where can we go that would be fun, and oh by the way, do you know any great babysitters? You share that information, that person will share it with you; it's something of value to them and they want you, somebody they trust and love, to have it. Hopefully that information will be as useful or as pleasurable to you as it was to them. Or sometimes you'll be on a business trip, get in an Uber, and ask the Uber driver for tips about local restaurants or places to see because they obviously know the area and you trust their response.

But today, thanks to the digital world, I can ask those same questions online, and get *millions* of responses within minutes from our followers. What a fantastic tool! Their information might be just what I needed, despite the fact that I've still never had any real personal level of engagement with them like I do with my family and friends.

With social media, strangers share with strangers. In fact, they're *expected* to share. You can read ratings and reviews of tiny guesthouses in Ethiopia or Iceland or Tasmania you'd never have known about (and that make you want to get right on a plane!), or about a novelist who's just put out an amazing book, or where to buy the loveliest wooden knitting needles and yarn. You can speak to people who have certain medical conditions and get advice from them in addition to what your doctor is telling you. You can find people with amazing parenting advice, too. This kind of sharing makes the world feel both intimate and comforting.

Shaun and I have used this network of information and people several times. After we decided to adopt a second time, we were having a hard time finding the right agency to work with. We asked our online followers which agencies they had used, why they liked them, and asked for more advice. Within a few days we noticed that one agency name kept popping up over and over. We asked more questions of these people via direct messages this time and soon had enough info to confidently begin the process with that agency. Within a few months we were matched with Paisley's mom and a few months later had a sweet baby girl in our arms. Without our network of followers online, we would never have found this particular agency and thus never have found Paisley!

With Daxton's diagnosis of ADHD and later autism, we have relied several times on information we have found in online communities to learn about food, medicine, therapies that work, doctors, or numerous other subjects. It's also been so helpful to know that we aren't the only parents experiencing certain behaviors or dealing with the frustrations of having an exceptional child. More than once, my soul has been buoyed by reading others' info and realizing we are *not* the only parents experiencing that!

*Over*sharing, on the other hand, can quickly get out of hand. I believe there are two types of overshare. The first is the daily-life overshare. This is mostly benign info that just really isn't pertinent to anyone, tweeting about how you just got done shopping for new underwear, or endless gym selfies, can be examples of oversharing when done constantly. The second type of overshare has to do with what I think is often an emotional reaction, or overreaction, when you're upset or frustrated. Whether it's venting about something that other people may feel differently about or making pointed or hurtful comments to others, especially strangers, because their comments have irked you in some way, we see a lot of this on Facebook today.

People are, of course, entitled to their feelings, but it's important to draw the line at intolerance for other people's positions or opinions. Equally important is figuring out how to check the incessant need to post your own position about it.

As a result, we have had the overshare conversation more than a few times in our house—mostly when the teens are upset at our parenting and venting to friends. Or when they are upset by a teacher for giving a bad grade on a paper, or a friend for some other reason. We want them to feel their feelings, but when they get too personal or too lopsided in their recounting (as teens will often do), we have had to remind them that it's not okay...even if they are justifiably mad or upset.

We deal with the oversharing syndrome in the comments on our YouTube channels all the time, too. (I'll discuss when this turns into bullying in Chapter 11.) I always tell my girls, "If you don't like the way someone is dressed, you don't need to say that to them. You're entitled to the opinion—but you aren't entitled to state it. Not everyone needs to hear your opinion or your instant thoughts."

BAILEY, ON OVERSHARING

I think oversharing about daily life happens so often now that it's almost like nobody makes a big deal out of it. When social media was newer, it might have been different, and certain posts may have seemed odd, but it's such a common occurrence now that it's no longer such a big deal. Which is bad in a way, but people are so used to everyone sharing everything online, that it's almost like you are not sharing at all because most people don't even pay attention to it. You're just scrolling, clicking, scrolling, and on to the next!

NUANCE IS SO IMPORTANT

One of the hardest things to deal with in terms of digital communication is nuance. With any form of written-only communication, all face-to-face communication is gone. Your body language and gestures, the emotions on your face, the tone of your voice—not there. Context becomes much harder to judge. It can quickly make a small situation that could easily have been resolved in person into a large and painful situation. Saying something sarcastically, for example, can be shrugged off with a wink or a laugh in person, and whoever you said it to will "get it" and move on. Typing something sarcastically when you're trying to make a joke can fall flat, and all the explanations in the world won't matter to someone whose feelings have been hurt.

I've been told before that I'm an angry texter. Ha-ha! I'm really not, but apparently I type very succinct, short, and efficient texts. I don't spend time on the details. In my defense, I'm almost never really upset...I just have a thousand things on my brain, and my mind is quickly jumping from one to the other so I write a short, crisp text and send it off. I've had to learn to slow down a little, reread my texts, use more emojis, or even end with "Know what I mean?" so that people can better read my emotions. My teens tell me that emojis are imperative for this as they can help relay with a wink or a thumbs-up that my text was informal and lighthearted where my words inadvertently may not do that.

I worry a lot about how much time kids spend on their phones—when they're in the same house, or even the same room! It feels like they're not as savvy at dealing with people in real life, or as they'd say, IRL. Many studies have shown that when these kids go off to college and are wholly responsible for themselves for the first time, they have to rely on a lot more analog behavior than they're used to as digital experts. It can be very stressful for them, and a lot of them have a hard time coping. Written communication is what they've come to prefer, but that doesn't help when you have to cook your meals or do your laundry or get to class on time. That certainly wasn't an issue when I went to college, of course, because everyone was as analog as I was!

I believe that the most effective form of communication is the one you do jointly with your eyes and your ears. The moment you eliminate the ears part, you're only relying on the eyes—and you've lost half of your ability to communicate. I tell this to my kids all the time, especially after I look at the phone bill at the end of the month. The log shows me how much data we've used and most of it's due to all the texting. And I know how many times my teenage girls text—it's in the *thousands* every day with their friends and boyfriends and school pals and whatever. I'll say to them, "When was the last time you actually called them on the phone?" They look at me. They give a side smile. Then they go right back to texting!

I try hard to get my kids to spend more time working on their face-to-face communication. Of course, they spend all day in school with their peers, but as soon as they're home, out comes the cell phone. Having specific times set up when cell phones aren't allowed, like dinnertime, is helpful. I even have friends that do "phone fasts" with their kids and set aside a week here or there throughout the year when their kids can only get online for one hour a day. Usually this is over holidays or other times it won't interfere with schoolwork, but it again reminds the kids that they can actually survive without their phones—*and* it forces them to interact with other family members the old-fashioned way.

For the last couple of years, we have gone on a vacation to a mountain cabin for a week or so to get away and spend time with family. Cell reception is nonexistent in the mountains, and every year I watch as my kids complain and whine about being bored and not having anything to do for the first day or two without their phones. But just like clockwork, on day three, my kids start getting creative. Suddenly the card games come out, the interactions pick up, the family talent shows begin, and forts start being built out of blankets inside and sticks/trees outside. The kids begin to play outdoor games with their siblings/cousins/friends such as capture the flag, hostage, geocache, or hide-and-seek. And every year when we leave, they talk about how much fun they had and that it's one of their favorite trips. Works every time!

BROOKLYN, ON CELL PHONE ADDICTION

I don't think our entire generation is addicted to social media per se—it's just because our cell phones have so many tools on them that we use in our day-to-day lives that not having them would be like taking a stove or microwave away from someone's kitchen. People don't know how to make their food without a stove; we don't know how to set an alarm without a phone or communicate with our friends without texting!

I also feel like there's more pressure to always have your phone, because your friends always seem to assume that if you're not getting back to them, it's on purpose. That even happens with parents a lot. There's definitely a contradiction where parents are trying to teach their kids moderation and they keep telling you that if you're having personal time with a friend, then don't spend all your time on your phone, but then parents get mad when kids aren't answering their text messages or their phone calls when they're out and about.

You need to compromise. Maybe send a text that says, "Hey Mom (or friend), I'm going on a date. I'm not going to be on my phone for the next couple of hours. Just an FYI if I don't get back to you." Just remember to do that to avoid unnecessary drama!

SOCIAL MEDIA IS AN INCREDIBLE WAY TO CONNECT

Social media creates community. Just watch the way the world comes together when a tragedy strikes. Twitter and Instagram will immediately be filled with a hashtag about the event where anyone can find information, words of condolence, encouragement, or ideas for how to help. Celebrities and people of influence can proclaim their support and amplify ways to get involved. Worldwide fund-raising is real-time and spreads quickly. Entire movements for good can be started by simply creating a relevant hashtag and sharing with your friends. With social media, we are more aware of what is going on in the world, more likely to take care of each other, and more likely to participate in social good.

Brooklyn: "One of the most interesting things we've ever done on social media was with some of our viewers. We have a group message going in our Instagram direct messages, and we popped in every once in a while to talk to them. One night we scheduled a virtual sleepover where everybody was online for a few hours, and we were all texting as if we were able to talk to them in person, and they were asking us all kinds of questions. It meant so much to them—and to us—to have that personal connection with them. A lot of these teen girls were confiding to us about problems with boys, or being self-conscious, and we always try to respond with positivity and encouragement. We are just like them, going through the same stages of growing up, and it is okay for them to know that."

Bailey: "Often, we get comments on our Instagram page from our followers who tell us things like, 'Y'all are the only thing that makes me smile every day.' Or how we help them get over their depression. That always makes us feel good about what we're doing!

"We love using our social media platforms to help others. We've used them to raise funds as UN Foundation champions for its Girl Up program, and to raise money to give girls in poverty-stricken countries an easier access to education. As a family, we gave up our Christmas last year and raised additional funds for a water purification project in the Dominican Republic. That facility will provide clean water to over five thousand people, as well as funding microbusinesses within the community using the water facility's profits. We've even raised awareness for causes like the Bill and Melinda Gates Foundation, female empowerment, teacher appreciation, and many other programs. With so many wonderful examples from others, it just goes to show you that you *can* use the Internet to share goodness and help influence the world with positivity, too!"

Kamri: "One day I was tagged a bunch of times by followers of my Instagram account, on posts that announced that one of the owners of a Brooklyn and Bailey fan page was diagnosed with cancer and was only given a short amount of time to live. I told Brooklyn and Bailey and we quickly got in contact with her mom and sent her a video message that we recorded, telling her we were sending prayers to her and that we wished her well. The girl was *so* excited to receive the video and posted that it had made her very bad days a little bit better! She later passed away due to the disease, but her mom was so grateful for us and for the ability we had to help make her daughter's last days just a little less terrible. And she made us stronger, too."

Rylan: "I like seeing all the GoFundMe posts popping up in my feed. I feel good knowing that people are using the Internet to help others who are in need. I also like using my social platforms to cheer on my sisters or other family members, like when I posted asking people to help Kamri hit one million followers on her IG account. It made me feel good to know that I helped her reach her goal."

Daxton: "One time in my coding class, a boy made a mistake with his work online. The other boys were making fun of him through comments in our program and I told them to stop bullying him. I sent him a note through the program we were using and told him I liked him, and I am glad we are friends."

Paisley: "I don't have social media! Does this mean I get a YouTube channel? But I like reading the nice comments from people when I am in a video or my mommy posts pictures of me."

THE DUBAI CONNECTION

One of our most wonderful social media experiences took place when we went to Dubai during spring break a few years ago. Lots of You-Tubers do meet-ups in the United States, but not many make an effort to go to other countries. We knew from our analytics that we had a pretty strong base in the Middle East, so when we decided to go to Dubai for spring break, we thought a meet-up might be fun.

After we arrived and got over our jet lag, we posted on Instagram that we'd be in a public park frequented by locals for a few hours. For safety reasons, we announced the flash meet-and-greet only shortly before it was scheduled to happen. Based on the comments on the post, we thought fifty or even a hundred people would show up. When we arrived, we found approximately fifteen hundred teen girls and their families waiting in line.

We were a little overwhelmed by the number since we hadn't brought anyone or anything to help with crowd control. Brooklyn and Bailey had never seen so many people eager to meet them. We situated the girls, and the meet-up ended up being *fantastic*. Just like hair, the family is universal. There were burka-clad moms chastising their children and wagging their fingers at them just like I do! When these moms saw that we needed help keeping a line together, they quickly formed a barrier by holding hands to ensure that Brooklyn and Bailey wouldn't be overcrowded. When they saw a couple of dads trying to cut in line with their daughters, they got fierce and sent them packing. Some American tourists who came to see the girls also helped control the line. It really is a small world: A guy in a Texas T-shirt came over to help us, and we later discovered we have dear friends in common.

It was so moving to watch. It was nearly a hundred degrees outside, and the locals kept bringing the twins Popsicles, cold drinks, and fans. By the end, we had countless bouquets of flowers. I realized later that the flowers were an even greater sign of respect than I had first thought as it's difficult and expensive to grow flowers in the desert. Many of the girls we met were wearing hairstyles they'd learned from our channel, and they were all completely thrilled that we were there.

That amazing day showed us the true power of social media. It was all about goodness, sharing, and caring for others. The parents I met loved their daughters enough to bring them to a park in the sweltering summertime to meet a few Americans they'd only seen in videos. We didn't speak the local language, but it didn't matter. Social media had brought us together, and we were united in love for each other and family. Hugs in these instances have meant the most to us.

Acknowledge the risks of social media, but don't let fear convince you that the bad outweighs the good because, in fact, the opposite can be true. It's like hearing the emergency instructions at the beginning of a flight. You need to listen carefully, of course, but afterward, you can sit back and appreciate that the plane that's taking you to a new and exciting destination is quite safe. If more people use the Internet and social media to spread positive, uplifting messaging, it will continue to become better and better.

The amount of kindness our family has seen, the fun opportunities we've been offered, and the heartwarming memories we have created are truly a blessing for us all.

Chapter 3

Rules and Contracts for Using Social Media and Cell Phones

The easiest and most foolproof way to make clear and to enforce family rules is with a written contract. We first created one when Brooklyn and Bailey were turning twelve and were given their first cell phones, and I can't imagine not having them. The rules are clearly spelled out, and if they are "accidentally" forgotten, all you have to do is pull out the contract and refresh the kid's memory! This makes it easier for everyone to know what's expected of them and what the consequences will be if the rules are broken. Feel free to use any of these verbatim, or create your own contracts based on your family's unique needs. Remember to always cover rules for children *and* their parents. This is a mutual trust agreement, not a dictatorship.

Also, when making rules to regulate your kids' devices, take your time figuring out what you want to include. My contracts are quite explicit and detailed, but that doesn't mean yours have to be. I just include as many details as I can so we have very specific conversation points with the kids. This ensures that they understand almost every possible scenario before they encounter it. But don't make rules you know deep down that you can't or won't enforce. You need to stand firm, be explicit, and of course, stick to the rules yourself, especially with a rule that is likely to be unpopular. See Brooklyn's sidebar on phone tracking on page 146, and you'll understand what we mean!

Ask older kids for input; you may want to have a short-term contract to see how well it goes. If circumstances change, be flexible and add an addendum to your contract or draw up a new one. For example, on our contracts we set a shut-off time for cell phones and other devices. This is crucial not just to keep kids from sending messages when they're tired, but also so that their bodies can slow down and get ready for a restful night's sleep. But as the kids got older, we realized they *needed* to be on their phones or computers to do homework, since their schools only accept digital files (talk about a shift from our analog days!), so we had to extend the hours when homework had to get finished.

Even though we have rules and contracts, kids will always test our limits! *Your* job is to be the stern but loving enforcer. Not the friend. Not the mom or dad who loves their kids to bits and lets them get away with things they shouldn't because it's easier and really what's the harm? Nope. You are the social media sheriff—and don't you forget it!

OUR CELL PHONE CONTRACT

When we gave Brooklyn and Bailey cell phones when they were twelve, it was the first time we allowed them access to digital media without it being thoroughly supervised. I knew that cell phones could present a myriad of problems and experiences that my kids might not be prepared for. I'm a list maker by nature, and started to create a list of things I wanted to discuss with the girls before they could have their own cell phones. I searched the Internet for ideas, too, and found other parents offering suggestions on what to discuss with their kids. Before long, I realized it would be easiest to simply create a contract that we could all go through together, discuss, and formally sign. I hoped having it in contract form and signed by them would allow them to own the consequences for bad behavior and prevent them from being angry at me and Shaun later on. Pulling out the cell phone contract elicits an eye roll every time, but it does work, because I can use the contract to remind them that they did, in fact, know the rules and still chose to break them. They also knew what the consequences of that decision would be.

CELL PHONE CONTRACT

The following contract between _____ and _____ seeks to establish family rules and consequences regarding cell phone usage inside and outside of the home.

CHILD RESPONSIBILITIES

Phone Care

____ I understand that I am responsible for knowing where my phone is at all times, and for keeping it in good working condition.

____ I understand that I am responsible for paying for a new phone should I lose or damage my current phone.

____ I will keep my phone charged at all times.

General

_____ I will keep my phone password protected at all times.

_____ I understand having a cell phone is for the purpose of communication with my parents, and therefore, will answer any and all calls from my mom or dad or text/call them back immediately in the event of a missed call.

_____ I will not go over our family plan's monthly minutes or text message limits or data usage. If I do, I understand that I may be responsible for paying any additional charges or that I may lose my cell phone privileges for an undetermined amount of time.

_____ I will not use the data on my phone without permission from my parents and understand that if I do, my parents can opt to turn off my data at any time.

_____ I understand that texting should not replace in-person interactions with people. I will continue to make efforts to socialize IRL, make personal phone calls, or go on physical outings with friends and/or dates.

_____ I will not install any app without prior consent of my parents. I promise to never install a vault app, or any other app that specializes in hiding Internet surf history or any media content.

_____ If I am asked to put the phone away, I will do so immediately and without eye rolling and/or mean-spirited comments.

_____ All of my phone's "Contacts" must include the full name (not nicknames) of the contact as well as the phone number and be approved by my parents. (In other words, not just "Sherrie" but "Sherrie Ward)".

____ I will not let my friends use my phone, especially out of my presence, unless I have a legitimate reason for doing so and with prior consent from my parents.

____ I understand that having a cell phone can be helpful in an emergency, but I know that I must still practice good judgment and make good choices that will keep me out of trouble or out of danger.

____ My parents must be able to access my phone and know my password at all times, and I understand they can spot-check my texts/group messages/tweets/surf history, etc., at any time without warning. I hereby agree to comply immediately and without eye rolling and/or mean-spirited comments.

____ I understand that my parents may opt to install apps on my phone that monitor my texts or e-mails until they feel I am mature enough to handle them on my own. I also understand that I cannot bypass or uninstall these apps without permission.

____ I recognize that this contract is subject to change via my parents at any time.

____ I acknowledge that for the purpose of this contract, the word TEXT can also mean Tweet, DM (Direct Message), GM (Group Message), Snap, Kik, iMessage, e-mail, IG Message, or any other electronic means of communication via my cell phone or apps on my cell phone to another human.

Rules/Etiquette

____ I will not bring my cell phone with me to the family dinner table.

___ I will not talk on the phone during family conversations or when at family events.

___ I will not text or place phone calls after 10 p.m.

___ I will not idly surf the Internet or use unnecessary data due to boredom. I will find something else to do.

___ I will leave my phone in the kitchen overnight, starting at 10 p.m., and will not take it to my bedroom.

___ I will not pull out my phone and casually surf or text while someone is talking to me.

___ I will obey any rules my school has regarding cell phones, such as turning them off during class, or keeping them on vibrate while riding the school bus. I will also not check my texts during school or other activities in which texting is deemed inappropriate by my parents.

___ I will make sure my phone is turned off when I am in church, in restaurants, in theaters, at funerals, or in other quiet settings where cell phone use is not appropriate.

___ I promise I will alert my parents when I receive suspicious or alarming phone calls or text messages/Snapchats/pictures/etc., from anyone, whether I know them or not.

___ I will alert my parents immediately if I am being harassed or bullied by someone via my cell phone or social accounts.

___ I will not use my cell phone to threaten or bully anyone else or participate in mean conversations, gossip, or have unkind words toward or about others.

___ I will *never* give out my name, address, phone number, parents' names, school information, or other personal information via the phone without express permission from a parent.

___ I will refrain from talking on the phone very loudly or very near other people.

___ I will refrain from discussing personal subjects on the phone in public.

___ I will refrain from texting other friends when I am spending time with a specific friend, as it may cause me to be aloof or disconnected or possibly hurt feelings.

___ I understand that text messages don't always portray feelings and intonations correctly. I will make every effort to use emojis to express my feelings so my comments are not misinterpreted. I will also make an effort not to make statements that can be confusing or open for interpretation.

___ I understand that texts can be screen-grabbed and so I will refrain from writing anything my parents, pastor, or principal wouldn't approve of.

___ I will not text or talk on my phone while driving.

___ I understand my phone tracking should be on at all times, and that my parents may monitor my whereabouts with it at any time.

___ I will send no more than _____ texts per day.

___ I will not answer any calls or reply to any texts unless I know who it is and it has been approved by Mom and Dad.

___ I understand I am not allowed to delete text logs without permission. This is vital.

___ I understand that my parents have permission to reply, call, e-mail, or text any of my contacts/messages at any time.

___ I will not change my settings or passwords without express permission from my parents.

___ I will not send embarrassing photos of my family or friends to others. In addition, I will not use my phone's camera to take embarrassing photos of others. If I receive such photos from someone else, I will notify my parents immediately.

___ I will not text about others when I am angry and realize that texts sent in the heat of the moment are often the ones I will regret the most later.

___ I will not allow geotagging on any photos or apps without permission from my parents.

___ I will not download or install any apps without first discussing with my parents and reading all the terms and conditions so I understand what abilities I am enabling the apps to do on my phone

Consequences

___ I understand that having a cell phone is a privilege, *not a right*, and that if I fail to adhere to this contract, my cell phone privilege will be revoked.

___ I understand that my cell phone may be taken away if I talk back to my parents, I fail to do my chores, or I fail to keep my grades up or use my phone for any questionable or illegal activities.

___ I understand that I may lose my phone if I am bashing my parents or family members in texts to friends or others.

___ If I am asked more than twice to turn off or put down my cell phone, or if I use it during "no cell" times, I will lose my phone for a day. I can lose it for as much as one day for each time I do not put it away when asked. (This amount can change if needed.)

___ If I fail to correct my behavior after _____ times, I acknowledge my parents' right to remove the phone from my possession until they decide that I am mature enough to follow the contract.

PARENT RESPONSIBILITIES

___ I understand that I will make myself available to answer any questions my tween/teen might have about owning a cell phone and using it responsibly.

___ I will support my child when he or she alerts me to an alarming message or text message that he or she has received.

___ I will not display undo anger when my child reports a problem or makes a mistake as long as they are honest about said issue.

___ I will model good cell phone behavior to my children by also abiding by the above rules of etiquette in regards to cell phone usage, and their respective consequences.

___ I will alert my child if our cell phone plan changes and impacts the plan's minutes or data.

___ I will alert my child if the fees or cost of the phones changes and he/she must begin paying for some of the recurring charges.

___ I will give my child _____ warning(s) before I take his or her cell phone away.

_____   _____
(Child's Signature)   (Date)

_____   _____
(Parent's Signature)   (Date)

_____   _____
(Parent's Signature)   (Date)

THE NIGHTLY RAID

In our house, we have what the kids dub the Nightly Raid: Shaun and I take the phones, devices, and computers away when they're being used past the time specified in the contract. If they are caught with phones after hours, they know they will lose them for a few days…or much longer if there have been multiple infractions.

The thought of getting their phones taken away strikes terror into my girls! Their entire lives seem to be ruled by their phones. Without their devices, they can't get notifications about schoolwork or announcements about drill team practice, and they miss messages from their friends. Most of their school classes require phones to access Google Classroom or online textbooks so not having a phone can really hurt. It's great motivation for kids to earn their phones back and to demonstrate better cell phone behavior.

If you don't want to physically remove devices from bedrooms, there are plenty of apps that allow parents to cut off Wi-Fi and data to cell phones. This allows the kids to keep the devices in their rooms and use them for alarms, but shuts off texting and Internet after set hours.

We started the Nightly Raid on electronics use after 10 p.m. (times may adjust depending on age) because—even if they deny it—teens are *tired* by then. When they're too exhausted to think clearly, it's easier to send a message that they'll later regret. We all know how easy it is to make errors of judgment when we're overtired, and it's up to us, as parents, to protect our kids from saying or doing anything they probably wouldn't have said or done had it been earlier in the day.

We do make exceptions to the raid only when there is a tremendous homework overload. Along with so many high schools in America now, our kids' schools send assignments online. Textbooks and classwork are all online and can't be done any other way. (So much for great penmanship!) In addition, text notifications are sent detailing where to upload homework and other assignments. We simply can't take away phones and computers when our kids need them for schoolwork. Be careful, though, that your kids aren't saying that they need to study when you later find out their "need" was to be Face-Timing or texting their friends!

Shaun: "When I was growing up, one of the most cherished items in our house was our grandma's encyclopedia set. The bookshelf full of hardcover books organized alphabetically served as our only access point into any topic of information we wanted to or needed to research. Any and all prep for homework assignments came straight out of these books—they were the Google of my generation. I was thrilled when I went to college and could suddenly get the whole set on a CD instead of having to go to the library to do my assignments. What a time saver (and shelf saver!). Our kids have *no* idea how lucky they are that one touch of a search button gets linked to all the research and sources they could possibly need, and that even the best research libraries didn't have when I was in college. The great part about this is that there is easy access to information for schoolwork. The bad part is that it is a bit too easy to be able to look up answers instead of actually doing the work (and in the worst-case scenario, plagiarize the sources)."

Another extremely important point you likely know already is how electronics and the light they emit are detrimental to proper deep sleep.

Not only do all kids need to physically unwind before bedtime, such as with a nice hot bath or shower, but they need to turn off anything with a screen. Studies are showing that the specific spectrum of blue light emanating from electronic screens can mess up a body's proper release of melatonin, the body's natural sleep hormone, and trick your brain into thinking it's not dark outside, making it so much harder to fall right asleep. (You know this is true as cell phone manufacturers have coded a user-enabled dimming feature upgrade into their operating systems that can take effect any time the phone senses a low light situation.)

Don't forget that the Nightly Raid applies to *you*, too—it's only fair that this rule should be enforced for everyone in the household.

BROOKLYN AND BAILEY, ON THE NIGHTLY RAID

Brooklyn: I used to hate my phone curfew!

Bailey: Me, too!

Brooklyn: The thing that drove me nuts was that in the beginning the phone curfew was like 9 p.m.—but I didn't often get to sleep before midnight. And then, my outside curfew was 10 p.m., so I couldn't even use my phone when I was out and that just drove me insane. I could just never use my phone after hours and that used to aggravate me so much, but I've gotten more used to it. At least our phone curfew is now 10:30 p.m. It's just so frustrating, since I also read my books on my phone and I watch TV shows on my phone. There are just, like, so many things that can be done on a phone now. I put my phone down, and I'm, like, what do I do now? [*Mindy:* The analog mom in me laughs out loud!]

Bailey: When my phone goes away at curfew, I actually go to bed and get some sleep. I like my sleep.

RYLAN, ON LOSING HER PHONE PRIVILEGES

When Rylan finally got her first cell phone, she read through and agreed to our family cell phone contract. She had the phone for only a few months before she lost her privileges after three serious strikes. Whenever we give our kids their first phone, we anticipate that there will be a few minor infractions and we use these as opportunities to teach and guide them. But with Rylan, the infractions just kept coming on a daily basis. Using her phone past curfew turned into prolonged text messaging when she was supposed to be doing homework. She would also sneak down after she'd gone to bed and take the cell phone from our kitchen counter (where we charge the kids' phones at night) back to her room and play app games into the night. The final straw was when we spot-checked her text threads and found that she was saying some mean things to a friend of hers. At this point we realized that despite her being the same age as our other kids when receiving her first phone, she was not ready to be responsible for it yet. So we took her phone away for several months.

Rylan knew she'd messed up, and she dealt with it really well. What we realized was that she ended up having much more of an analog summer, like Shaun and I used to have when we were kids with no access to telephones. Back then, we'd go over to our friends' houses to see if they were available to play with us, and if they weren't home, we'd troop on back home, and as Rylan put it, "Be bored all day!"

Rylan: "It was kind of annoying over the summer because I always had to go to my mom's phone to text my friends. If I needed anything when I was out, I would have to beg my friends to let me use their phones. In this neighborhood it's a mile to walk to my friend's house, which isn't that bad, but when I'd ask my mom about it, she'd always be, like, "Go ask her yourself." I couldn't text her from my own phone and I don't have a bike, so I would have to walk or Rollerblade all the way down to her house. But then she wasn't home that much—she'd be out somewhere with her mom. So I'd have to head all the way back to our house and have nothing to do. I was happy when school started again!"

After six months, we had Rylan reread her contract and write a paper on why she felt she deserved her phone back. She gave thoughtful responses, so we decided to return her phone and again set out to determine whether she was ready for the responsibility. And she proceeded to show us that she was!

OUR FAMILY COMPUTER CONTRACT

Each family needs to determine at what age their kids may begin to use the computer and when/if their kids are responsible enough to have their own computer. This contract was created after I spent days online researching all the possible problems kids can encounter when they first begin using a computer and enter the Internet unsupervised. There are so many potential problems, it can be overwhelming!

This contract became especially useful to our family when it came time to discuss all these different scenarios, as we had a template for very open, frank conversations about the various pitfalls kids can stumble into online. You'll notice that some of the terms are very similar to our cell phone contract—but that's okay. It's better to define conduct even further in a contract, rather than being less specific, and be ready to adapt and make changes as the kids get older and more mature.

THE MCKNIGHT COMPUTER CONTRACT

The following contract between _____ and _____ seeks to establish family rules and consequences regarding computer and Internet usage.

CHILD REQUIREMENTS

Computer Care
_____ I understand that I am responsible for knowing where my computer is at all times, and for keeping it in good condition.

___ I understand that if using a laptop, I should never leave it lying where it can be stepped on or damaged or stolen.

___ I understand that I should transport my computer in a protective cover or backpack at all times.

___ I understand that I should avoid eating or drinking anywhere near the computer.

___ I understand that I should avoid touching the screen whenever possible and should clean the screen regularly.

___ I will only use computer-safe products to clean the keyboard, mouse, screen, etc., and if I am unsure what that means, I will ask for help from a parent.

___ I understand that I am responsible for paying for a new computer should I lose or damage my current computer.

___ I will turn my computer off at night and when I'm not using it, to avoid wasting electricity.

___ I will enable automatic operating system updates to keep the health of my computer up to date.

General

___ I will keep my computer password protected at all times.

___ I understand having a computer is for the purpose of communication with my parents, teachers, coworkers, etc., *or* for the purpose of doing homework and gathering research information off the Internet.

___ I will always use the computer in a public room in the house, and promise to never use the computer behind closed bedroom doors.

___ I understand that I may be responsible for paying any fees I incur for any online shopping or accidental downloads, etc., *or* that I may lose my computer privileges for an undetermined amount of time.

___ I will not use the computer without permission from my parents and understand that if I do, my parents can opt to take away my computer from me at any time.

___ If I am asked to put the computer away, I will do so immediately and without eye rolling and/or mean-spirited comments.

___ I will refrain from using any messaging platforms without express permission from my parents and then the same rules will apply as with my Phone Contract.

___ I understand that having a computer can be helpful and necessary for school, but I acknowledge that I must still practice good judgment and make good choices that will keep me out of trouble or out of danger.

___ My parents must be able to access my computer and know my password at all times, and I understand they can spot-check my computer or messages at any time without warning. I hereby agree to comply with this immediately and without eye rolling and/or mean-spirited comments.

___ I recognize that this contract is subject to change via my parents at any time.

___ I acknowledge that for the purpose of this contract, the word TEXT can also mean Tweet, DM (Direct Message), GM (Group Message), Snap, Kik, Message, e-mail, IG Message, or any other electronic means of communication via my computer or apps on my computer to another human in the universe.

Rules/Etiquette

____ I will not bring my computer to the family dinner table.

____ I will not use my computer after 11 p.m. without permission.

____ I will not use the computer in my room without permission.

____ I understand that, generally speaking, the computer should stay in the common area of the house to prevent overuse, misuse, or possible problems.

____ I will not use my camera on the computer without permission. All other times that I use the computer, I will place a nontransparent piece of tape over the computer's camera lens to prevent hackers from accessing the camera.

____ I will *never* give out my name, address, phone number, parents' names, school information, or other personal information via the computer without express permission from a parent.

____ I will not post or send pictures or other content that will embarrass me, get me into trouble, or jeopardize my privacy or security. If I receive such posts or photos from someone else, I will notify my parents.

____ I will never agree to meet anyone I have met online without permission from my parents. If I meet them, I will need one of my parents with me and the meeting will need to be in a public location.

____ I will not enter any chat rooms or other forums without permission from my parents.

____ I understand my parents will be installing a network safety system that will limit my access to material they feel is not appropriate. I will use this system and will not complain or try to find ways around it.

___ I will not idly surf the Internet or use the computer to waste unnecessary time gaming, etc.

___ When a pop-up banner or ad comes up, I will not click on it but will click out by using the X. If an inappropriate ad comes up, I will notify my parents immediately.

___ I will not use a credit card to purchase anything off the Internet without my parents' permission.

___ I will not download any software or games even if they say they are free.

___ I will be a good online friend and be supportive of my friends and others who might be in trouble or in need of help.

___ I will make sure my computer is put away when I am in quiet settings or public places where computer use is not appropriate.

___ I will obey any rules my school has regarding computers, such as turning them off during class, or keeping them put away while riding the school bus.

___ I promise I will alert my parents when I receive suspicious messages or see alarming behavior from anyone online, whether I know them or not.

___ I will alert my parents immediately if I am (or someone I know is) being harassed or bullied by someone via my computer.

___ I will not use my computer to participate in mean conversations, gossip, other unkind acts, or bullying people in other ways. I also will not send threatening or mean e-mails to others.

___ I understand I am not allowed to delete sent e-mails without permission.

___ I will not change my settings or passwords without express permission from my parents.

___ I will protect my passwords and practice good Internet security.

___ I will be thoughtful in my use of copy, paste, and forwarding. If I use anyone else's content or images, I will quote them, give them credit, and link to them if appropriate.

___ I will not break any copyright rules by using text, music, video, or images that don't belong to me without permission.

___ I will read and understand how to use CC and BCC in e-mails and be mindful of not sending out lists of contacts' personal e-mail addresses to other people without permission.

___ I will not send embarrassing photos of my family or friends to others. In addition, I will not use my computer's camera to take embarrassing photos of others. If I receive similar photos of anyone else via my computer, I will immediately notify my parents.

___ I will not use my computer to edit videos or photos in such a way that would hurt or embarrass myself or anyone else.

___ I will not use my computer to look at pornographic material, visit gambling sites, access pirated media, etc.

___ I will not use my computer to search for anything dangerous or illegal.

___ I will not remove my browser history without my parents' permission. I will also not use incognito or private browser windows without my parents' permission.

___ If they need my help, I'll assist my parents, teachers, or others in their use of technology.

___ I will respect other people's digital property and space. I won't steal, hack, break into anyone else's accounts, or use another's content or personal information without permission.

___ I will use clean language online.

___ I will not enter restricted 18+ age sites.

I understand that online:

___ People are not always who they say they are.

___ People don't always tell the truth.

___ There is no such thing as privacy.

___ I may interact with inappropriate material that is not my fault. When this happens, I should notify a parent or guardian immediately.

___ Being behind a screen does not give me permission to be rude, unkind, or say hurtful things. I may disagree with people but I don't always need to say what I'm thinking.

Consequences

___ I understand that having a computer is a privilege, *not a right*, and that if I fail to adhere to this contract, my computer privilege will be revoked.

___ I understand that my computer may be taken away if I talk back to my parents, I fail to do my chores, or I fail to keep my grades up or use my computer for any questionable or illegal activities.

___ If I am asked more than twice to turn off or put down my computer, or if I use it during "no computer" times, I will lose my computer for a day. I can lose it for as much as one day for each time I do not put it away when asked. (This amount can change if needed.)

____ If I fail to correct my behavior after three times, I acknowledge my parents' right to remove my computer from my possession until they decide that I am mature enough to follow the contract.

PARENT RESPONSIBILITIES

____ I understand that I will make myself available to answer any questions my child might have about owning a computer and using it responsibly.

____ I will support my child when he or she alerts me to an alarming e-mail or instant message that he or she has received.

____ I will not display undo anger when my child reports a problem or makes a mistake as long as they are honest about said issue.

____ I will model good computer behavior to my children by also abiding by the above rules of etiquette in regards to computer usage.

____ I will give my child _____ warning(s) before I take his or her computer away.

____ I will make or find a list of recommended sites, or bookmarks, for my children to visit.

____ I will seek out safe options for Internet monitoring which may include possibly blocking and filtering inappropriate content for my children.

____ I will try to always be aware of my child's online friends and "buddy list" contacts, just as I try to get to know their circle of influence in real life.

____ I will frequently check to see where my children have visited on the Internet, via their Internet history.

___ I will set reasonable rules and guidelines for computer use by my children and will discuss these rules, posting them near the computer as a reminder. I will monitor my children for compliance with these rules, especially when it comes to the amount of time they spend on the computer.

___ I will not overreact if my child tells me about a problem they are having on the Internet, but will work with them to solve the problem and prevent it from happening again.

___ I will report suspicious or illegal activities to the proper authorities.

___ I will put the home computer in an open family area of the home.

___ I promise not to use a computer or the Internet as an electronic babysitter.

___ I will provide my children with opportunities for other types of entertainment and recreation involving outdoor and/or physical activity.

_____   _____

(Child's Signature)   (Date)

_____   _____

(Parent's Signature)   (Date)

_____   _____

(Parent's Signature)   (Date)

BROOKLYN, ON THE COMPUTER CONTRACT

One of the rules included in the computer contract said that if you did not take care of your computer, then you had to pay for a new one, or go without if it was broken. When I had my first computer, I would often toss it or leave it on the floor next to my bed after doing homework late into the night. One day, in a rush to get ready for school, I stepped on my computer and completely cracked the screen. I was incredibly upset but I had to face the consequences of my actions, and for several months I went without a computer, doing my homework on the family desktop, which was old and had a major lag. Eventually I earned my parents' trust back enough to ask for a replacement computer for Christmas, and by contributing some of my own money to buy it since the broken screen was my fault. I learned through this experience the value of taking care of your things, and paying attention to the computer contract rules.

Chapter 4

Social Media Basics: Tips, Hacks, and Everything You Need to Know

If you're going to have a *child* online, you need to be a *parent* online. Your children have been born into a digital world. They are completely at ease with developing technology and are constantly networking with each other. Even if you're not interested in using these different platforms, the only way to keep up with your kids' tech savvy is to become proficient yourself. Specific platforms will come and go, but basic tech knowledge is a must—you have to master the digital world before it masters you! Otherwise, you won't be able to guide and teach your kids how to judge what's good or bad for them.

Most important of all is your ongoing involvement in and dedication to anything your kids participate in. It's not just knowing about apps and online platforms—you need to be *on* them. You need to see who's following your children and you also need to see what your children are posting or sending out. You might be shocked or even horrified, but more than likely you might be delighted and thrilled by what amazing things your kids can do.

Using social media is a digital online journal of sorts. Tweens/teens use it to express themselves and their life moments. I've enjoyed watching my kids develop their own sense of style, personality, knowledge, or love of others via their social media. When Kamri first opened her Instagram account, she took the basic selfie-type pictures that are standard for most teens. But over time, Shaun and I watched as her picture styles began changing. Different perspectives were added, different colors, and macro photos with tons of detail. Soon we saw her playing with various apps to edit the photos before she posted them. Detailed pics of butterfly wings or leaves facing a sunset began to pop up occasionally, all with the use of expert depth of field and lighting. Seeing her love for the art of photography, we bought her a nicer camera and started to teach her how to use aperture, ISO, and shutter speeds to play with the compositions of her photos. Today she continues her love for all things photographic and has a natural talent and ability for editing and taking photos. She just turned fifteen, which is very young to acquire the photography and editing skills that all started from her simply taking photos on her phone to post on her social media.

SOCIAL MEDIA ETIQUETTE

Despite the fact that our children are more fluent in social media than we are, we should still be having conversations with them about social media etiquette. Rules about manners and etiquette need to be as clear for online communication as they are for real-life situations.

Why is this so important? The online world exposes you to literally billions of other people. You never know who's going to be reading or watching what you post on the other end—which means think before you share.

And, of course, there is no off button. Social media exists 24/7, and what was once confined to school, your house of worship, your workplace, or the walls of your home is now accessible everywhere. Because there is so much activity at any given time and it occurs in such short snippets, I constantly wonder what effect this is having on my kids' attention spans. Our kids' generation has become so used to making snap judgments based off instant info that often this takes over their ability to pay attention, concentrate, and study. These snap judgments can have a profound effect on their decision making and the accompanying consequences. This makes basic rules about etiquette even more important.

In addition, nuance is also tough. It's too easy to misinterpret a text or a posting in a way you'd never misinterpret a conversation because you can't hear the other person's tone of voice, see their body language, ask what was meant, and clear up any misunderstandings.

Shaun: "When I was a teenager, you had your inner circle of friends, your acquaintances in the next circle, and then everyone else in the periphery. What type of connections did I have with those groups? My close inner circle was usually a group of five to ten people who'd hang out or play sports together, and we talked to each other all the time—as in, actually *talked*, face-to-face or on the phone. Then there were acquaintances I saw every once in a while outside of school or my typical circle of friends from church or the neighborhood, or said hi to when I passed them in the hallway. Today, thanks to social media, a typical teen will have hundreds or even thousands of friends in their 'inner circle' because they watch each other's feeds closely; that makes them feel like they 'know' each other. All these friends/followers can see what others ate, what they did today, and what their test scores were. If they like what someone else posted, they put little hearts on it or make a comment. Back when

I was a teen, there were no more than a dozen people in my inner circle, but today, if a thirteen-year-old kid decides to post a video showing how to blow doughnuts with the smoke from a vape, hundreds of people are watching. It's as if he took a bag of feathers and shook them out so the wind would take them—if he changes his mind about sharing the post, he'll never be able to get them all back into the bag.

"That's why posting without really thinking can be so dangerous, which we'll discuss in more detail in the next chapter."

Anonymity Is No Excuse

It's extremely easy to become anonymous online, and some users say or do things they'd never dream of in real life when they think there won't be any consequences. Don't let anonymity tempt your kids into irresponsible commenting/posting. A screen does not give anyone a license to be rude or mean *or* a license to post anything they may regret later.

One very important age-old saying in our family (and yours, I'm sure) is: "If you don't have anything nice to say, don't say anything at all." Online, this translates to: "Don't say anything online to a person that you wouldn't say to their face."

We also tell our kids, "If you wouldn't say it in front of the Three P's, don't post it online either." For us, the Three P's are your parents, your pastor, and your principal.

Shaun: "We know that if we were able to meet some of the people who may have made negative comments about us, our family, or other YouTubers or social media influencers, we would find that they are probably genuinely really nice people. It's just you get them in a position where they know they're likely never going to be found out, so they say what they really think. Is this negativity doing the world any good? No, it's not. But we all have bad days or get angry or frustrated about something we read online, and feel the need to comment to make ourselves feel better without thinking about the impact it might have, which often isn't benign at all.

"We want our kids to know that they have a choice. The twins have a large audience, but as individuals, they get to choose whether to put out good or negative messages. They know that what their followers see on their feeds has a ripple effect, and they strive to produce constructive content and to promote that effect. Their followers become role models for good manners and good ideas to their own peers. To borrow one of the twins' favorite hashtags from our church, #sharegoodness.

"In other words, we know that we can train our audience (to some degree) on what kind of content to expect from us and those in our spaces. When we are kind and share goodness, they will, too. When we delete hurtful comments or gently remind people that this is a safe place, it's quite amazing and wonderful to see how our audience begins to monitor the space for us. When this happens, children are also learning by seeing positive etiquette online, and what is or isn't appropriate.

"It is also hard to convince tweens and teens, who tend to live in the moment, about the dangers of posting things that can come back to haunt them in either the near future or years later. In one case that received extensive media coverage in October 2017, a cheerleader at a Utah high school convinced her friends to say two highly offensive and racist words backward, and they filmed themselves laughing as they said the words over and over. The video went viral and the backlash was deservedly fierce as the school said it would take 'appropriate action.' What she thought was a joke wasn't, and while details are scarce about the final 'action' taken by the school, the story will remain online in perpetuity—meaning any college or employer Googling these students will be able to read about their 'prank' and judge them accordingly."

BAILEY AND BROOKLYN, ON NEGATIVITY AND NEEDING A THICK SKIN

Bailey: I'd have to say the best thing about social media would be our family's experience on YouTube. We have what I call a self-imposed filter on what we put up because there's always that rule of what's on social media always stays on social media. There's definitely some monitoring we have to do, but since our brand is really positive, we don't typically let negative things slide. But I still get surprised by some of the things that people say, especially on Twitter or Instagram or YouTube when people hate on others just because they're a public figure. I don't understand why you would take your anger out on strangers on social media. It just reflects poorly on you more than it reflects on the other person. Our rule is to never respond to hate with more hate. Either respond with kindness or don't respond at all. That goes for in-person communications or online.

Brooklyn: You need to develop a thick skin. I remember the first time I read a comment that was so mean that it actually hurt me. And my mom was, like, "No, they're just kids who don't know what they're talking about, or may be hurting inside themselves." Ever since then I just kind of look at it from that perspective and it really helps.

USING THE MOST POPULAR FORMS OF SOCIAL MEDIA

We have our own McKnight version of the Miranda rights: Anything negative or inappropriate they post online can and will be held against them! Kids learn from an early age that everything they say has repercussions—good, bad, or neutral. It's no different online than it is in the "real world." Having this rule in place before any social media connections take place is a great way to set boundaries and keep your children safe.

Just remember that all families will navigate and run their social media their own way—a way that might be the complete opposite of what you do. Some kids get cell phones when they're only eight years old, and have no trouble following the rules their parents set up for them; some kids get a cell phone at fifteen and abuse their privileges seemingly overnight. Some toddlers are managing iPads regularly and are masters with their favorite apps, while other much older children still need total supervision. Believe me, you'll be changing your ideas as quickly as new apps are released!

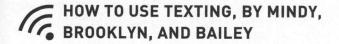 ## HOW TO USE TEXTING, BY MINDY, BROOKLYN, AND BAILEY

How It Works

Texting is a fast and easy way to communicate between smartphones and mobile devices by simply typing words, emoticons, or GIFs. (A GIF is an endless loop of a soundless video file, usually no longer than two to six seconds.) All smartphones have a texting app or feature (whether SMS or iMessage). However, there has recently been a surge in the creation of texting apps, especially for large groups such as GroupMe.

Who Uses It

In 2018, just about everyone uses texting whether it's kids/teens, the working professional, or even your grandparents.

What It's Used For

It seems like in today's world, texting has nearly replaced phone calls. It is a quick way to communicate between two or more people by simply typing what you have to say with words, abbreviations, and photos.

How Long the Information Lasts

If you're like me, text messages seem like they last forever because I never delete them, so they turn into very long threads! Text messages last for as long as you want to keep them, especially when backed up on your computer. When you decide that you no longer want or need to see a text, simply swipe or press delete to remove the text thread. There is also a feature in your phone settings that allows you to choose how long your messages will save to your device. For example, you can choose "delete after a year," and as the year rolls over, all texts older than a year automatically archive.

Other Features

The world of texting is constantly evolving. You can share music, photos, and videos. You can pay friends electronically via apps such as Venmo, send payment requests and confirmations via text through Apple Pay, and even play group games. If you have a smart watch, you can even send and receive your texts on your wrist!

How Can It Be Shared?

Texts can be shared and screen-grabbed between smartphones/cell phones and mobile devices (e.g., tablets, laptops, smart TVs, and even game systems).

Can You Save What You Post?

Texts are automatically saved in your phone in a thread organized by contact name. You can search for certain threads by clicking on the search bar at the top of your text app, and search using a specific person's contact name. Often, people will screenshot a text thread to remember certain things or to share a conversation with a friend.

What Can Go Wrong

There is always a chance you could send a text message to the wrong person, which can be troublesome. The biggest issue is when you are in areas of poor service; the text messages won't send, making it difficult to communicate. Lastly, what you send out digitally will always exist out there in the world digitally. There is no way to fully take back an errant text, or a text containing inappropriate content, which brings us to our next point.

Can You Change Your Mind?

Unlike e-mail, there is no way to unsend a text message, other than turning off your phone or quickly flipping it into airplane mode and wishing and praying for it not to process. Certain phones such as the Apple iPhone have a text feature known as "Invisible Ink," which allows you to send messages that disappear after they are read. However, if that person takes a screenshot of your message, your content will forever exist out there.

Keeping Your Account Private

Privacy when it comes to text messaging is relatively easy. Just don't share your number with anyone you wouldn't want to have it. You can always use the block feature if you don't want a contact to be able to text you. An alternative to using your personal phone number is to download a texting app (or use an alternative phone number). Using parent apps to monitor cell phones can help parents keep their kids from using texting apps without their knowledge.

Tips and Tricks

- Know how your kids' phones work. This is an amazingly simple point, but so many parents don't understand all the little tricks cell phones now have. Either go to a phone store or set up a walk-through education session online or on the phone to answer any questions.
- Turn microphones off for privacy. There are lots of rumors about AI (artificial intelligence) listening in on convos right now and feeding you certain ads based on that. We will eventually learn more about these AI listening tools, but for now, you need to protect yourself.

DIGITAL IS AN ENTIRELY NEW LANGUAGE

When you were in English class in high school, did you ever imagine that you'd be punctuating messages with emojis and abbreviations? I didn't—because they didn't exist! But if you want to be as fluent as your children are online, you need to know the most common shortcuts and digital language usage. Don't panic if you don't know the text lingo right away—you can always look up what various acronyms mean. These are the ones we see most often:

- Sexting = sending X-rated images or messages via text.
- Emojis = those little images that replace words that communicate emotions, etc.

- Streaming = downloading media to watch.
- LOL, WTG, ROFL, BTW, RN, KWIM, etc. = laugh out loud, way to go, rolling on the floor laughing, by the way, right now, and know what I mean.
- Trolls = No, they aren't imaginary goblins that lurk under bridges, but people who "troll" others online to leave comments that are usually negative or derogatory.
- Bots = computer-generated fake accounts and/or replies to messages, usually found on Twitter or Facebook.

HOW TO USE SNAPCHAT, BY BAILEY

Snapchat is like the naughty child of social media. You post what you want, knowing it will be gone in ten seconds. I struggle with it because of that aspect—any platform that allows something to disappear after it is posted breeds the opportunity for something bad to happen. Especially as you can take a screenshot of any post to archive it, which negates the instant good-bye.

How It Works
Snapchat is an app for mobile devices that allows you to chat with your friends. You can take a picture or video, add filters that alter how the image looks, and send it to any of your friends on the service. The videos can't be longer than ten seconds, and the pictures can be seen for only the same short time. You can also send text messages.

Who Uses It
Mostly teens/tweens or digital influencers.

What It's Used For

Teens use Snapchat to communicate and share pictures and videos. A lot of teens use it as a way to send images and messages they don't want people to have permanently. I text my mom and my family, but if I'm going to talk to my friends, Snapchat is what I use. I post stuff on Instagram but don't chat with people there.

How Long the Information Lasts

Snapchat is different from other social media because the messages sent through it are designed to disappear after being read. Any message, photo, or video you post will be gone for good in ten seconds. Your stories will last for only twenty-four hours. Snapchat does make it harder for a potential employer or college recruiter to find images. If someone decides to save the information by taking a screenshot of an image or a message, the sender will automatically be notified that a screenshot took place.

Other Features

Snapchat has features called Memories and Stories. In addition to sending messages directly to other users, you can also take a picture or video and post it on your Story, which is like a newsfeed that any of your friends on Snapchat can watch. The images last for only twenty-four hours; once that period is up, the posts disappear. That is where Memories come into play. If you want to save a snap that you have taken, you can save it to your camera roll by clicking a button in the bottom left corner. When you do that, the snap is automatically added to your Memories, which are accessible on the app itself.

Another fun feature is Streaks. This is when you and a friend also on Snapchat both text each other back within one day. Basically you've messaged each other every single day, and the longer that you do, the longer the streak is. So the goal is to keep the streaks going. Streaks can be so important to some of the kids that they'll leave their phones with their parents when they go to summer camps where they can't have their phones, and their parents' assignments are to keep their streaks going!

How Can It Be Shared?

Snaps are sent just like messages. They are shared with whomever the sender wants to send them to.

Can You Save What You Post?

Yes. See "Other Features," above. You can also screenshot other people's snaps, but they are notified when you do so. There are ways around this. For example, if someone wanted to save something that was on Snapchat but he didn't want the person who snapped it to know, he would grab my phone and screenshot the snap onto my phone, and then text it to himself—the original poster on Snapchat would never know. Or if you have a separate digital camera, you can do the same thing by taking a photo of your screen. There are apps that specialize in saving screenshots of snaps.

What Can Go Wrong

Because they are under the impression that what they send will "disappear" after ten seconds, teens might use this social media platform to send images of things they would not usually share, such as pornography, talk of suicide, drugs, sexting, bullying, crimes, etc. But screenshots can be taken and distributed via Twitter or Instagram. There are also websites and apps that allow users to save snaps without notifying the sender. As you already know, the Internet is forever, even when you think it isn't!

Can You Change Your Mind?

If you send someone a post, you cannot delete it or take it back before they see it. Content posted to Stories can later be deleted.

Keeping Your Account Private

You can change your privacy settings to control who can see your stories. Unlike Instagram, where users often have multiple profiles, Snapchat users generally have only one account and regulate who can see it by refusing friend requests.

HOW TO USE INSTAGRAM (IG), BY MINDY, BROOKLYN, AND BAILEY

How It Works

Instagram is an app that allows you to share photos and videos to an online following. Like Facebook, the posts from those you follow will show up in a feed. Instagram also offers Stories, which allow you to create short bursts of video updates throughout the day that disappear after twenty-four hours.

Who Uses It

Instagram is mostly used by tweens/teens and Millennials (but it seems that working professionals and parents are also joining the bandwagon!). People who are into fashion, fitness, and beauty tend to use Instagram the most. It is also heavily used by brands and digital influencers as well, as a way of marketing products and/or services.

What It's Used For

Instagram is a way for users to share their lives via photos and videos. However, it seems like IG has really transformed in recent years. Now you can use it to discover lifestyle, beauty, traveling, art/music, and DIY content. In many ways, it's become the new Pinterest in terms of generating ideas for people looking to improve in certain skill sets such as decorating, culinary arts, fashion, etc.

How Long the Information Lasts

Your IG posts live forever in the app until you choose to either delete your account, or delete an individual post. Instagram Stories last for only twenty-four hours, and Instagram Live lasts for as long as you are using the live feature. You can save your IG Live videos afterward, and choose to have them shared to your IG Story. (Once again, just because you delete an image in Instagram does not mean that it is erased from the Internet.)

Other Features

Instagram Stories—Instagram Stories allows you to capture and post moments throughout the day without posting to your main profile. These posts last only twenty-four hours, and automatically delete after that time is up. You can add fun filters and text/stickers to your story directly through the app, just like Snapchat. They are now also being automatically archived (unless you turn that feature off) so you can repost or reuse them. You can also link a website to your Instagram story. Influencers and brands use this to promote products and give their followers a chance to learn more about the subject of their post.

Instagram Live—Instagram Live allows you to capture and broadcast moments of your daily life in real time, whether it's a concert, a special event, or a chill day at home, and allows followers to tune in and comment live. You can also save and add your IG Live to your IG Story after your live broadcast has ended.

Instagram Direct Message (DM)—Direct messages allow you to share text, images, and videos to select followers/users.

Discover—This feature allows you to find new content/accounts, or popular/trending content.

Instagram Highlights—Keep all your old stories in subject-specific buckets on your profile by clicking any story into the Highlights feature.

How Can It Be Shared?

You can share your Instagram posts by clicking to share to your other social media accounts when you post the photo, opt the link, and text/e-mail it.

Can You Save What You Post?

You can save your Instagram posts. There is even an option to have them saved to your camera roll. There is also an option to save someone else's post as well. Just click and hold the ribbon button at the bottom right of the picture, and save it to a playlist. You can go onto your profile and view your playlists with those saved pictures anytime. Instagram story pics are auto-archived unless you opt out.

What Can Go Wrong

There is always the possibility you could upload the wrong photo, DM the wrong person, post on the wrong account, or even share something you regret later. You can always delete your posts or messages; anything that you've ever posted online, however, will always be available somewhere, so be careful what you post!

You can also inadvertently fall into feeds of photos you don't want to see such as partial nudity or other obscene content. Sometimes the Instagram Discover feature can be the most dangerous content in this regard, especially if you have young children. Certain hashtags will also bring up questionable photos. Instagram does try to filter out explicit pornography, but some people take it as close to the line as possible, which can be dangerous.

Also, sometimes your phone's geolocation may be turned on, and you are not aware, resulting in your photos being coded with your physical location on them, making where that photo was taken available to all who view the photo or video. Make sure this feature is turned off on all your devices.

If you're worried about what your kids are searching for, check their Explore page on their Instagram accounts. Go in and submit as spam anything "bad" that pulls up, as this helps prevent that info from coming up all the time. This also tells you what your kids might be searching for since each person's Explore page is unique to their searches. (For example, my Explore page has a lot of hair pics because that is what I'm commenting on or viewing all the time.)

Can You Change Your Mind?

If you change your mind, you can simply delete the post.

Keeping Your Account Private

In your settings, you can select to have a private or a public account. Private means that only people you choose to accept can see your account. All other follow requests you can deny. Public status on your account means anyone can see it. You can also choose to select specific followers with whom to share your IG story and even choose to hide your posts from certain followers.

Tips and Tricks

- Make sure that Internet use in your house is in a public place, in full view of everyone, and apply content filters if necessary. We have a little cubby off our living room so that we can easily supervise our kids when they go online. They know the door has to stay open. This is harder to do when your kids are teens and want and deserve privacy. I always say that trust is slowly built and easily lost and that phones are a privilege and not a right. As you'll read about in more detail in the next chapter, I still believe older kids require random spot checks on their devices. They'll never feel immune to the consequences of what they post because they understand that, at any given moment, Mom or Dad can take the phone and check what's going on. Most of the time, we're pleased to see that nothing is amiss, and the kids get a pat on the back and a reminder that we love them.

- For younger children, one way to stay looped into their social media is to *only* allow them to access their social accounts on a parent's phone. This is a good way to monitor what they're up to before you really want to give them a phone.

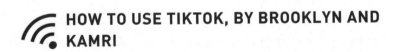 HOW TO USE TIKTOK, BY BROOKLYN AND KAMRI

How it Works

TikTok is primarily a skit and lip-sync music video social app to create short-form videos. Viewers can "heart" your videos and follow your account, which can help you get discovered by new users.

Who Uses It

Anyone can use the platform, but it is mostly used by kids, tweens, and teens.

How Long the Information Lasts

Videos last forever after you've posted them, unless you delete the post. Live moments will last only twenty-four hours after they have been posted.

How Can It Be Shared?

You can share by copying the link, texting or e-mailing it, or saving it to your camera roll. You can also share on other social media platforms.

What Can Go Wrong?

There's always a chance someone may steal your content, but if you keep an eye out it's easy to make sure nothing like that happens.

Can You Change Your Mind?

Yes. At any point you can change your privacy settings on your account, or delete past posts.

Keeping Your Account Private

In your account settings, you can choose to share content with friends and family only, or with the public.

 HOW TO USE STREAMING, BY SHAUN, MINDY, BROOKLYN, AND BAILEY

How It Works

Streaming takes place via an online service or app for mobile devices that allows you to listen to music or watch TV shows, YouTube videos, movies, or even live broadcast videos wherever you are. Some streaming services require a monthly subscription, but there are many free (and legal) services as well. (Illegal sites stream copyrighted material, such as films, without permission, and are often linked to computer viruses.)

Who Uses It

Most services require you to be a certain age to sign up for an account, but nearly anyone can use streaming services at any time whether you are at home or on the go.

What It's Used For

Streaming is an easy way to have millions of entertainment options at your fingertips no matter where you are, whether it be music, movies, television shows, podcasts, etc.

How Long the Information Lasts

Streaming lasts for as long as you run the app session or hold a subscription to the service. Streaming services may choose to remove, add, or filter content, which can affect the content that is available to you. For example, Netflix and Hulu add and remove movies and shows every month in order to keep the content on their platform relevant and fresh. Streaming services may also offer different content based on your location; Netflix suggests different movies and shows to their subscribers in India vs. the United States, etc. That said, platforms such as Spotify and YouTube offer the same content around the globe based on the user's interests.

Other Features

Streaming has an array of features. Depending on the service you are using, you can create playlists, share with friends, and more. With music streaming specifically, you can listen to music even when you don't have Wi-Fi. YouTube just announced last year the ability to watch videos offline. Other streaming apps allow you to have access to music videos, live videos, TV shows, and more. If you are really loving a song, the app can direct you to where you can buy it. Some apps/services allow multiple people on the account or give you the option to buy a family plan so everyone can share and enjoy their favorite entertainment.

How Can It Be Shared?

If you are really jamming, or enjoying a show, you can share with your friends and family through the streaming service whether it's via text message, social media, or even within the app.

Can You Save What You Post?

Some streaming apps allow you to add, save, or download content for as long as you have your subscription or account.

What Can Go Wrong

Not much can go wrong, except for what my dad says in this section. Ads are typically present on these services and can be annoying, but most services allow you the option to pay for an ad-free service. Of course, if you don't have unlimited data, you have to be Wi-Fi-dependent, which can lead to streaming connection issues. This can become incredibly expensive.

Shaun: "Streaming is one of the best ways to use the Internet, as so much content—music, movies, TV shows, podcasts, YouTube videos—will literally 'stream' to be instantly watchable on your device. But there is a huge caveat to live streaming that scares me—which is how much damage it can unwittingly do.

"In the other platforms we use, particularly YouTube, we film our scenes and then edit them to make our videos as engaging as possible. Editing allows you to add all kinds of features as well as catch mistakes, like a misstated word or something that might be misinterpreted, and gives you the opportunity to cut them out. While with live broadcasting, there are no do-overs, edits, or censoring, so whatever you or your kids say will be out there forever. We've allowed our kids, who are experienced at putting content online, to go live occasionally, but only if we as parents are there to supervise.

"Another danger to live streaming is that hackers can easily find out your location through a live feed by listening to environmental noises or by looking at your surroundings. Some unscrupulous pranksters have gone so far as to call 911 when someone is live streaming, to report a crime in progress, just so they can watch the police arrive and see what happens to the innocent victim. Never mind that this is a felony and a dangerous waste of police resources (and has sometimes ended up with the innocent victims being harmed and mistaken for criminals).

"A lot of kids do live broadcasts and say, 'Okay, you can ask me anything!' The good thing is that, with yourself or your kids, if you say, 'Ask me anything,' who's really in control of where the direction goes? It's you, right? Well, if it's your children who are involved in this, you know they could be asked some inappropriate or too-personal things and you know they want to be genuine, and they could answer the question and it could lead into something that you don't want discussed. So I think it's important for a parent to be involved in that process if their kids are going to broadcast live. I also think going into it, if you say, 'Ask me anything,' give strict guidelines about the topic, such as 'Ask me anything about our family vacation.' Teen commenters have been known to cross the line and say things like, 'Can you take off your shirt—hey, you said ask me anything!' You don't want that happening to your child."

We have very strict guidelines with our kids about going live. Our kids aren't allowed to go live without permission first, and when they do, they need one of us parents to be on the stream when it is taking place. This allows us to make sure we are all comfortable with the setting, fully aware that they are live, and can monitor what is discussed. We ask our kids not to film near the mailbox, the front of the house, or other places that might identify where we live. We often ask them not to wander the entire house while filming so that people can't figure out the general layout of the house. We have the notifications on our phones turned ON so that on the off-chance any of our children do go live without permission, we get notified and can jump into their live streams and watch what is happening. If the live is on Instagram, we ask them to turn off their public comments before going live (if your account is already set to private, this isn't a problem). If someone goes live and has the public comments turned on and their live starts trending, it will be pushed to the Explore page on Instagram. When this happens, you can get lots of creepers leaving nasty comments or asking for inappropriate things. Using this setting to limit comments to only your followers or only people you follow will prevent this from happening.

There are also filters under the same settings on Instagram where you can add swear words and other words you don't want to allow posted from viewers during the live. We add in our phone numbers, our address, etc. Remember to misspell a few of the worst words as this is a common workaround for filters.

Can You Change Your Mind?

The nice thing about streaming is that you have autonomy. If you don't want to continue with the entertainment, you can change it, or unsubscribe from the service altogether.

Keeping Your Account Private

If you are not in the mood to let everyone know what you are streaming, you can easily switch your streaming mode to private to ensure that no one can see what you are doing. In addition, you can always disable any settings that would post to your social media accounts. You can also set up specific password-locked child accounts for younger children in many of the streaming apps. This allows you to keep certain types of content (PG, PG13, etc.) out of those locked areas and only allows your children access to content that you are comfortable with.

 HOW TO USE SKYPE OR FACETIME, BY MINDY

How It Works

Skype and FaceTime are services that allow you to keep in contact with your loved ones or colleagues through a video call. If you have an iPhone, you can FaceTime anyone else who has an iPhone, Mac computer, or iPad. For Android phones, there are apps called House Party, Cabana, Google Duo, or use Facebook Messenger. The Skype app works on all devices, as long as you sign up for an account. To use it, you have to download the app on your mobile device or log in online. Simply search for or select a contact and you can video-call that person.

Who Uses It

Anyone can use it…kids, parents, grandparents, family members, coworkers, boyfriends/girlfriends, BFFs, and more.

What It's Used For

Have a long-distance friend or bae (that's short for "before anyone else," or babe)? Business colleagues in another country? Skype and FaceTime are ideal, as well as any other teleconference software. Kids love it as it enhances their calls with full visual communication, too. It's the convenience of calling anyone with the added bonus of actually seeing their faces, reading their expressions, almost like you're talking to them in real life.

How Long the Information Lasts

The video call lasts for as long as you want. Simply click the end call button and the call will terminate.

Other Features

If you are not in the mood to video-chat (bad hair day?), you can select an "Audio Only" version, which allows you to communicate just as if you were making a phone call except that you do not need a phone plan. All you need is a Wi-Fi connection, so the call acts as a VOIP (Voice Over Internet Protocol) call. Some video-chatting apps such as Skype do allow you to communicate via text message as well, usually to leave a message in case the person you tried to contact didn't answer the video call.

How Can It Be Shared?

As of now, you cannot share your Skype or FaceTime calls.

Can You Save What You Post?

You cannot save your Skype or FaceTime calls either. However, there are apps that will allow you to screen-record your calls for later use.

What Can Go Wrong

Sometimes a poor Wi-Fi connection makes it hard to see the person on the screen or the video call can be dropped. People (especially teens) can also use the face-to-face calls for inappropriate activities such as video sexting, etc. This should be a huge concern for you as a parent, as we discuss in many different sections of this book. If you aren't using Wi-Fi, face-to-face calls will eat up a lot of data usage.

Can You Change Your Mind?

You can simply hang up the video call with the click of a button.

Keeping Your Account Private

You can manage your Skype account's privacy in the settings. For example, you can control who can make Skype calls to you, whether anyone with a Skype account can find you or only your friends and family who are listed on your direct contact list. Online safety is important and Skype allows you to both block specific Skype accounts or simply remove them from your contact list.

Tips and Tricks

- In the App Stores, any app that has already been installed on a device will have "Open" when you click on it. An app that hasn't been downloaded will say "Get" or "Buy." If you hear of apps that are inappropriate for teens and children, but can't find them on their devices, simply go to the App Store on their devices and search for a given troublesome app. If your child has ever downloaded it, you will see either "Open" or a cloud with a down arrow under it, instead of "Buy."

- Kids are fickle about the apps they use. They often download something, use it once or twice, get bored, and then delete it or forget that it's there. That doesn't mean you shouldn't be checking out what they check out. If the kids are excitedly discussing a new app, download it yourself. Get a family plan that requires users to ask permission before any app can be installed. This works for free or bought apps.

- Don't give your kids access to your credit cards. Check your bill every month to ensure that nothing has been downloaded without your permission.

SHAUN, ON WHAT TO DO WHEN YOU HEAR, "DON'T YOU TRUST ME?"

I grew up near a college town in Idaho, and I would always ask my parents if I could take the nicer car out on my dates, instead of the embarrassing minivan or old clunkers. My parents usually said no, and I'd ask my mom, "Why don't you trust me?" She explained that she trusted me and my driving skills, but she didn't trust the kids who went to the nearby colleges who came from out of state and didn't have a clue how to drive on icy country roads.

So it isn't that we distrust our kids. It's that we don't trust the world they're in to have their best interests at heart. Whether they're inside the house online or outside with their friends, that trust lesson applies.

When the inevitable "Don't you trust me?" line arrives, your reply should be something like, "Of course I trust you, but I'm not stupid!" Or something similar! The point you're trying to make is that, "Yes, I trust you, but I don't trust the Internet. I know that kids and teens might not have the judgment yet to make the best decisions when they get into situations. And I also don't trust the people who come into your orbit that you might not have control over." Just as my parents didn't trust the young inexperienced drivers in the snow.

VAULT APPS, BY MINDY AND SHAUN

How It Works

One of the biggest abuses of apps on cell phones is vault or ghost apps. These are apps designed to keep photos or information secret, and they're disguised as a perfectly innocuous app to fool anyone but the primary user about their real intention. In other words, they're deliberate digital hiding spots for stuff that kids should not be seeing or using. They can only be opened with a passcode that "unlocks" the vault.

Vault apps often look like calculators, clocks, or a simple video game. When checking their kids' phones, most parents just look at the text logs and social media feeds, and if they see a calculator, they're not going to think anything is amiss. Cell phones always come with default calculator and clock apps as part of the operating system, so seeing a duplicate function app is a tip-off, as is seeing a large file size on any app in this category in the phone's settings. You can also go to the App Store on your kids' phone and do a search for vault apps, looking for the "Open" or download-from-cloud icon as mentioned previously.

Who Uses It

Anyone who wants to keep information or images secret, mostly teens, particularly young boys and men who choose to hide pornographic content from family members.

What It's Used For

Hiding content and information you don't want anyone to see. Usually these will contain pornographic photos/videos, screenshots of text logs with sensitive conversations (sexting), cheat sheets for upcoming exams, etc.

Best Things to Use It For

There is *no* good reason for a child or teen to need to use a vault app.

How Long the Information Lasts

As long as the app is installed, the information will stay in the vault.

How Can It Be Shared?

The information or photos can be shared the same way anything can be shared from your phone, via Bluetooth, text, or e-mail.

Can You Save What You Post?

Vault apps are a repository, so anything stored there will remain until it's deleted.

What Can Go Wrong

If someone is keeping images such as pornography on his or her device, and they share any of it with minors, this is illegal. It constitutes child pornography. Teens often do not think of this as they are inter-sharing content among minors such as revenge porn, or candid locker room shots, etc. Some teen boys will even offer cash bounties to classmates in exchange for catching nude photos of a desired female, with their consent or not. The bounty goes even higher if the target female is a girl who would never consider taking a nude selfie.

Keeping Your Account Private

The entire purpose of a vault app is secrecy and privacy.

FOR THE ANALOG GENERATION ONLY

Ready for the eye rolls? Ignore them. Your kids will almost always shun apps their parents love and visit regularly. Most parents don't like the temporary nature of Snapchat, so that's where their kids are. Instagram, however, is becoming increasingly popular with adults, which will not make your offspring happy!

Facebook

My kids call Facebook "Deadbook"—because they wouldn't be caught dead using it. "It's for grandmas posting photos of their grandchildren," Brooklyn told me. Way to make me feel *old*!

I love to use Facebook to communicate with my friends. It's a terrific social media platform, making it easy to find long-lost classmates or acquaintances, get information and news, and join support groups. I also know it's the last place my kids will ever go to see what I've posted. It'll be interesting to see if our kids decide to join Facebook when they're older and start having families, and they realize what a helpful platform it can be. It may even be that Facebook reinvents itself and becomes relevant again to the younger kids.

Be warned, though, that oversharing on Facebook is a very common issue. It's incredibly tempting to post every cute thing your kids did, but remember, the Internet is forever. Your children are entitled to privacy, and as they get older, they might get upset to see something that you thought was adorable but that they find embarrassing or revealing. Even if you delete something, if someone has already shared it, it's still going to be available. I've read some postings on Facebook that were extremely alarming—talking in-depth about their child's very personal mental health issues or struggles with addiction, for example, without the teen's permission.

No matter who you are, it's important to be wary of strangers who want to friend you. If they have almost no other friends or photos on their profile, they're usually bots, hackers, or scammers. Be judicious in your friending. Some of these fake friends will hijack your account, send you viruses, post obscene content or fraudulent links, or hit up your close personal friends and family for money claiming to be you in an emergency (using info and names you have shared on your profile). You can report problems to Facebook or block users who are offensive, but Facebook's responses are often inadequate and frustrating, which is one of the site's biggest drawbacks.

Tips and Tricks

Always ask yourself if you need to share an image or an anecdote before sharing it. If you have any doubts, don't do it! Once the kids are old enough, ask their permission before posting. Or if they did give permission but ask you to take it down later, do it in front of them so they see that you value their opinion. Teens, especially, start Googling each other, and images they might have loved when they were ten can be deeply mortifying to them a few years later.

E-MAIL

E-mail is still the primary communication method in professional settings and the best way to write, receive, and archive longer messages, especially those with attached files. It's also harder when typing and sending e-mails to make mistakes that you might regret later. For kids, e-mail has been almost entirely overtaken by texting or tweeting. They use it only for school communication (if that) and see it as something adults need for their work.

We've found that we have to "teach" our kids to use e-mail! Despite how savvy they are with tech stuff, e-mail seems to be the one thing that they are totally disinterested in learning. We had to show them how to attach files, the difference between CC and BCC, the pros to using e-mails (such as having written, searchable e-mails), and more. We know as parents that professionals are still using e-mail, which means that we need to teach our kids e-mail proficiency before they leave for college. We started e-mailing project details to our kids or even forwarding their appointment reminders, college application links, etc., when they were juniors in high school. This process started slow, and over the next year we sent them more and more. In the beginning we even had to text them and say, "Hey, just sent you an e-mail!" That way we knew they would see and respond to it.

LANDLINES AND PHONE CALLS

Shaun: "I remember the day my parents brought our very first microwave home at Christmastime when I was about four. It was *huge* and probably cost a lot of money. In later years, I remember getting off the phone with my grandma, and I said to myself, 'Someday, the phone will have a TV in it, and we'll be able to see whomever we're talking to.' My kids have no idea what a revelation it is to people of my generation that we can do this on our cell phones. If I showed them the landline phone I used back then, they wouldn't know how to use it! I used to marvel at Michael Knight (from *Knight Rider*) being able to talk to his car KITT via his watch. Now I can make phone calls to anyone on my own smart watch!"

In many communities, landlines are becoming extinct, but it can be worth keeping one—not attached to an answering machine—as a safety measure for emergencies if you live in an area where your electricity is spotty. I have friends in New York City that keep their landlines because, on 9/11, regular phones still worked when cell phones were unusable. Having said that, our newer house doesn't even have any landline jacks in the walls!

If you have a regular phone, make sure your kids know how to use it, too. Recently, a company sent us a very cute lip-shaped landline phone. I showed the twins and mentioned that it would be fun to use it in a video as a prop. Bailey promptly picked up the phone and asked Brooklyn to give her a friend's phone number so she could call her. As I watched incredulously, she dialed the number, and her expression of sheer confusion when the phone didn't respond with a ringtone was priceless. "Bailey," I said, "the phone has to be plugged in to work." She looked at me as if I had two heads. I explained how, back in the olden days, telephones were wired to jacks in the wall because cellular communication networks didn't exist. Another my-age-is-showing moment for Mom!

It was kind of bittersweet, because when I was growing up, I spent hours and hours on the phone with my friends. The only privacy I had was stretching the corkscrew phone cord as far away from my siblings as it would go—I even hid in closets to chat with my girlfriends about my latest crush. Now, of course, kids text with blazing speed instead of talking, although it's a bit ridiculous to send twenty-three texts to try to make a date when a twenty-second phone call would do the trick. Girls will even text their boyfriends while sitting right next to them, rather than speak to them directly!

I worry a lot about this, as written communication is just not the same as in-person conversation. The subtle visual or aural clues you'd get face-to-face are impossible to convey with words only, so it's so easy to misinterpret something said in innocence, leading to drama and hurt feelings. Still, my teens prefer a text system. They claim it documents what was said, especially if the text is asking me for permission to do an activity, and they also say that it's faster. No chatty conversations that last forever with texts, they claim. They don't realize their three thousand texts are essentially the same thing!

MANNERS 101: RESPOND TO YOUR MESSAGES, PLEASE

Back in the olden analog days, if the phone rang, you answered it. If you missed a call, you returned it. Now, it's not so simple. So we decided to spell it out in our phone contract, which you'll see on pages 37 to 44 in the previous chapter, to make it so much simpler for our kids to understand and obey the rules about phone communication.

One of the rules is that if we as parents text them, they need to respond. Within reason, of course—if they're driving, then no texting, please! At their next stop, they can let me know the message was received. Or if you're really pressed for time, send an emoji. If I text the girls and say, "Hey, you need to be here at this time," and I can see that they've read it and they don't show up at that time, there are going to be consequences. If you establish mandatory expectations with Mom and Dad, this becomes a good habit with friend-to-friend communication. It really isn't that hard to interact in a timely, respectful manner! Our kids know that old cliché—what goes around comes around—is especially apt for texting.

Our three eldest kids have a lot of followers on social media, but we make clear to them how important it is to respond as promptly and as often as they can. It's impossible to answer everybody, but I tell them to be online often enough and reply to people often enough that fans understand that there's a chance that they *could* hear from you. (This is something a lot of celebrities forget, or tell their assistants to handle; often, they'll only respond when someone is attacking them or to pitch a product or service. Not a good way to keep your fans engaged!) We tell our kids that we want them to have a meaningful conversation with their audience. That being said, though, we also tell them that we do not want them to be on social media *all* the time.

About RnR

The flip side to this is RnR. No, this does not mean rest and relaxation as you would think! On social media, it stands for Read, no Reply. An example of this would be if I texted Brooklyn with a question and I could see that her read receipt showed she had read my text, but never replied. For adults, sometimes we just get busy and forget to respond to texts, but sometimes kids use this as an intentional way of hurting people. They know the other person sees that the text was read, but intentionally ignore them. This drives me crazy! I think it is so rude. Whoever does this is basically assuming power in the relationship and just blowing you off—on most social media sites, your followers and friends can see that you are online. RnR is incredibly passive-aggressive and causes endless hurt in many relationships.

Our kids know that their friends are sometimes really busy with schoolwork or other issues or personal crises when they don't reply. When that happens, a simple apology is enough. RnR becomes a difficult issue when it's chronic and meant to hurt the feelings of the person on the receiving end.

The best way to deal with this is to have your kids turn their "read receipts" off. It means they turn off the ability for others to see if they have read their messages. It also prevents hurt feelings for people who might think they are being ignored when you really are just busy or driving. To combat RnR, we as parents have to model good manners for our kids. If Mom and Dad aren't good at returning messages they receive, then their children are taught that ignoring people is okay. You don't want to answer rudeness with rudeness. Instead, you answer rudeness with kindness and good manners, which will eventually rub off on your kids and their friends.

Introducing a cell phone contract can help. Think about how you want your child to behave and what important lessons they need to learn in order to keep the privilege of a phone, which of course is what they use for all their social media communications. Friends respect each other. Everyone's time is valuable.

Ghosting

Ghosting is a step further than RnR. Sometimes, people simply stop all communication and disappear with no explanation—as if they've become ghosts to the friends they're neglecting because it feels like they just don't exist anymore. It's the modern-day blow-off. It's used a lot in relationships when people don't want to keep dating, but don't know how to tell the other person.

Sub-tweeting

Sub-tweeting is another passive-aggressive form of communication often seen on Twitter and other social media platforms. It's a post, often a tweet, that criticizes another person without actually mentioning their name—it's the digital version of the Carly Simon song "You're So Vain," where many of the people in her orbit thought *they* were the "vain" one! The person in question knows that their friend is talking about them, but doesn't have much recourse because they aren't specifically named. It gives the poster plausible deniability in case the recipient gets upset at the sub-tweet, by allowing them the reply that "You took my message out of context," or "I wasn't talking about you." A lot of kids, and even some adults, sub-tweet because they feel the need to vent or get back at a bully, but it often backfires and makes the situation worse. Kids are super-savvy, and they know when they're being talked about—or dissed.

For example, if Brooklyn tweeted, "Some people don't know how to make a punishment fit the crime," right after I'd taken her phone away, I'd know that she was talking about me. Could I prove it? No! She would look at me, smile sweetly, and say she was talking about her friends' parents. Shaun and I try to make our kids understand that sub-tweeting is not okay.

Strong Opinions

Thanks to the anonymity of the Internet, it's all too easy to share strong opinions without fear of censure. This trickles down to our kids, who can start to feel the need to convince everyone of their opinions and thoughts instead of agreeing to disagree or acknowledge they are both right. I think this is due to social media—and we certainly see it in our current political climate. Brooklyn and another cousin bumped into this over a college decision not too long ago, and it was tough to find a compromise when each was convinced she was right.

Kids are also more tuned into politics and world events than ever. Rylan asked me about who the president was when I was her age, and I didn't even know. As children, I don't think we paid as much attention to current events unless our parents told us something or we happened to see the TV news. Now kids are inundated with politics and current events via socials so they are very savvy and aware. The plus side is that it creates change, social movements, and solidarity (such as teenagers becoming invested in righting the wrongs of society with the #MeToo movement, women's rights, and other hot topics such as gun control and Black Lives Matter). The negative side is that it creates dissent, tension, and friends can be lost over differences of opinion. We always tell our kids that everyone is entitled to their opinion, but they can't convince anyone of anything who doesn't want to be open-minded enough to listen to ideas contrary to their own.

Acknowledgments and the (Dreaded) Thank-You's

Do you remember your parents' stern admonition to sit down and write thank-you's for all your birthday or holiday gifts before you even got to play with them? I do, grumbling all the way, of course!

Getting a thank-you note in the mail has become a rare occurrence now, but I'm digitally savvy enough to be okay with one that's e-mailed. But even that is becoming rarer, and it's more than a little upsetting when, for example, you give some very generous gifts and are met with...nada. For the dozens of wedding or graduation gifts we've given over the last few years, we've received only a few thank-you notes. It's so disappointing not to be acknowledged. Nowadays I think most people are fine with an e-mailed thank-you instead of a handwritten card. With teens, you'll be lucky to get a thank-you in a text message, and they'll make sure you know how long (as in fifteen seconds) it took them to write it!

So we make a point of ensuring that our kids send thank-you's whether by cards, e-mails, or texts. It's something we feel is part of our family culture, as well as our business, to acknowledge people and their efforts, simply because—we want everyone to feel welcomed and appreciated. We send out birthday greetings, and whenever we collaborate with other influencers, we try to send them a little something, like a fruit bouquet, as a thank-you for working with us. A small gesture can reap big rewards, too, as people always remember an unexpected gift and attribute it to you as a gracious person. It's not about what you send—but that you thought enough to actually send something.

We also love to do little things with our kids that are meaningful to each of them in a special way, so they feel that affirmation as well. I've sent little gifts to the girls at school at times, and I know that action has rubbed off on them. Once, when Kamri was having a particularly hard week and felt like she was the third wheel with her friends, Brooklyn overheard what was happening and called a cookies-and-milk service and had them deliver the goodies to Kamri at school. The note read, "See how many friends you get when they find out you have cookies!"

You always try to have an impact on your kids, and the most satisfying moments come when they show you what they've learned without you prodding them. As soon as Brooklyn got home, I told her how proud I was of her, and her face just lit up with joy. The life lesson had been learned, and she implemented it on her own.

So write/text/e-mail those thank-you's!

PARENTAL CONTROL

Two of the most popular and helpful smartphone monitoring apps I've tried are Our Pact and MMGuardian. These apps allow you to block certain phone numbers, view text threads, set usage time limits, and monitor what which sites kids are frequenting.

With the addition of iOS 12, Apple stepped up its parental control game with a new feature called Screen Time. So far, this may be my favorite monitoring tool yet. You can track how much time your children are spending on their phones, and see exactly what they're using. Using password protection, you can disable internet browsing and texting during a set time period (for example, during dinnertime or bedtime), even limit what music, podcasts, movies, shows, books, and apps they can use. Since putting it on Rylan's phone, Shaun and I see her pop up around the house much more often!

Expect immediate pushback when you first implement monitoring tools. But seeing your kids react negatively to your parenting means you are likely on the right track in terms of setting needed limits!

LIFE IS A MIX OF ANALOG AND DIGITAL—USE THE BEST OF BOTH

There are many things in life that kids will never be able to learn online. Ideally, you want to aim for that sweet spot where the best of analog and the best of digital seamlessly interface with each other, allowing your kids to thrive in the real world and the virtual one.

What can't they learn online? How to work inside the home. How to deal with other people socially. How to enjoy being outside in nature. How to do things with their hands and bodies that have nothing to do with electronics.

Don't be afraid to turn off the Internet. Have a Wi-Fi-free weekend at home every once in a while, or go camping where cell signals are weak. Some of our best vacations were cruises where there was no cell data onboard. I wish we could have more of this.

I am often in awe of how our kids are so much more adaptable and pliable than I was as a child—thanks to the wonders of the digital world, which makes them a valuable part of a global community. As you know if you've ever tried to learn a new language as an adult, it's not so easy to become skilled at something new, plus we tend to get more and more fixed in our habits as we get older. It's really wonderful that our kids are so at ease with digital technology because it's all they've known. They're the ones who are teaching us—as long as we're there to listen.

PART II

Family and Home Life

Chapter 5

The Family Structure

Now that you know all the important basics about social media, and how to set digital boundaries to keep your children safe and empowered, let's move on to setting up structures and specific rules to help you define your approach to parenthood that will allow your children to thrive.

I don't remember ever having a lightbulb moment when I realized I lived with family rules. They just always *were*. My mom once told me a story about when I was a teenager—someone had asked her how she'd raised such a nice girl, and I responded with, "I would never have dared try to have a wild party or sneak out of the house because I knew my parents would be so mad." My mom laughs about it now because she can see that parents really aren't all-powerful. If kids want to be bad and horrible, parents really have little control over stopping it. But rules in place give kids a healthy dose of structure and fear that helps keep them in line. Now that I'm an adult, if my kids tell me I'm strict, I often reply: "A healthy dose of fear isn't always a bad thing!"

Raising children and having a family are like a mini-ecosystem. When everyone is doing their job and being a contributing member, things can go well. When they aren't, things can quickly fall apart. In order to achieve this goal, we try to run our household much like the real world but on a mini-level. In the real world, your actions have consequences. Positive actions often have positive consequences, and negative actions have negative consequences. If you don't go to work, you don't get paid. If you study really hard for a test, you are more likely to receive a high grade as a result. In the real world, there are also responsibilities to other people besides yourself. There are laws you have to follow, such as rules of the road or standards of public conduct.

We try to create the same atmosphere inside our home but on a much more macro level. However, before we can do this, we need to establish the rules and philosophies that govern our mini-ecosystem. This is the moment when parents (or parent, regardless of what your family unit looks like) get to begin to shape their family structure. We use our family guiding structures—our family motto, our parenting philosophies, day-to-day rules, and individual responsibilities—to help shape that ecosystem and give our kids a foundation of stability to thrive within.

THE FAMILY MOTTO

Every family should have its own motto! It can be anything you like—short or long, funny or serious. A motto allows you to have something unique in it to define your family and make everyone feel that they have a loving place within it.

With any brand, you typically have a brand bible—your mission statement, your core values, your goals, your style guide, whatever these may be. Every decision you make as a business should tie back to highlighting one of those core values and furthering your company mission.

So the same thing applies with a family motto. All of the decisions that you make as a family should highlight and improve upon one of those core areas of your motto. Our own family motto is something we came up with from teachings in our church, in part, from *The Family: A Proclamation to the World*. Trying to get our kids to hold on to some of the ideals and tenets that we believe in, about loving God and loving others. Here it is:

As members of the McKnight family, we believe that family is ordained of God. Successful marriages and families are established and maintained on the principles of faith, prayer, repentance, forgiveness, respect, love, compassion, work, and wholesome recreational activities. Happiness in family life is most likely to be achieved when founded upon the teachings of the Lord Jesus Christ.

I think it's a very rare family that sits down and codifies what their family motto is, but once you take the time you need to really think about it, you'll end up pinpointing what's at the core of your values. This has helped us tremendously, in our private life and in our public platforms. Daily life can be chaotic as an adult, but having a motto can be an organizational structure to help you keep your priorities in line. It is also a way to make sure that you're teaching your children the rules and philosophy that you want to pass down to them. The earlier you start, the easier it will be to establish structure and rules as a normal part of the day. In other words, if being tidy is a core value, then your two-year-old should be expected to do certain chores, such as picking up toys or helping to empty the dishwasher (which, of course, they are perfectly capable of doing, and actually like doing at that age, especially when you make it a game!). Setting these expectations early means that by the time this toddler is a twelve-year-old, they'll know that chores are just a part of daily life.

That doesn't mean that our kids won't still whine and complain when we remind them that they haven't done their chores, but they know the structure of the home and its rules, and they know what the consequences will be if they're broken.

HOW TO CREATE YOUR FAMILY MOTTO AND PHILOSOPHIES

The Family Motto

A family motto is basically your family's secret sauce. It's the definition of where you want your family to go or to focus on long-term. For this reason, every motto will be different and have a unique flair to it. I've seen mottos that are only one word. I've seen mottos that are three words. I've seen a family whose last name was Roberts have a motto like "The Roberts family stands for: Responsibility, Respect, and Reason." Some mottos sound more like a philosophy, such as "Above all else, serve others." I've also seen mottos that are rhymes like "See, Say, Do, I love you." This one stood for if you wouldn't See it, Say it, or Do it in our home, don't do it outside our home. And I've seen mottos that are a full statement, more like ours. At the end of the day, the motto is *yours*. Figure out what feels right for your family and stick with it.

When people ask me how to develop a motto, I tell them to spend some time thinking about their family. What's important to them? What are the one or two or handful of things they really want their children to feel and understand deep in their bones? What would make them feel like they had failed and then use that information to focus in on what they want to highlight so they don't feel that way. If you found out tomorrow that you had one day left before you died, what is the information you would tell your family? Those questions are all good thought starters for creating a motto.

When creating a motto, don't be afraid to borrow from other people either. Don't stress about coming up with something totally original or choosing words that have never been used before. Our motto is from a widely published document our church uses. We just pulled different parts from different sections of that document and then put them together to create our family motto. A lot of the best parenting is taking golden nuggets of information from lots of people and then using those nuggets to create your own system.

The Family Philosophy

An adjunct to creating a motto is sharing ideas about the family philosophy—ideas and concepts you believe strongly that aren't rules but are important values that you want your children to learn. For us, some of the most important are:

- Travel as much as possible. It will expand your bubble and allow you to see beauty in diversity, cultures, and places.
- Give experiences, not things.
- Love everyone regardless of race, gender, beauty, sexuality, etc.
- Leave things better than you found them, particularly when outdoors or in nature.
- Work hard and play hard.

- If you don't believe in something, you will fall for everything.
- People might forget what you did for them, but they won't forget how you made them feel.
- Don't go to bed angry. Everything looks better after a good night's sleep!

Day-to-Day Rules

You can read much more about rules and responsibilities in the next chapter, but these are rules that still fit under the umbrella of your family's motto and/or philosophy.

For us, basic day-to-day rules are things like: You must make your bed. Pick up your toys when you're done with them. Don't hit each other. No swearing. Practice the piano thirty minutes a day. Get good grades.

Make a list of the rules you have put in place and you're set. Much like road rules or basic laws that govern our land, these are the rules that govern your family. You are most likely to hear these on repeat a hundred times a week. ☺

Individual Responsibilities

The rules govern the laws of the home whereas these define each person's role within that ecosystem. In our home, I do the grocery shopping each week while Shaun always handles the car maintenance or registration. We each fulfill individual roles that help keep the entire ecosystem running. Each of our kids has individual roles as well. Right now one of Rylan's individual responsibilities is to empty the dishwasher every day, while Kamri's is taking out the trash when it's full. Nobody else in the family should be responsible for those jobs, and if they aren't done, they land solely on the individual responsible. Everyone should have jobs that are "theirs," which they do simply because they live in the home, eat the food, and partake of the other benefits of that ecosystem. Even small children can have small responsibilities such as putting their own shoes on or making their beds.

THE CORE CONCEPTS OF OUR FAMILY

Core concepts are themes that start popping up in your family. I don't think we ever sat down and had a formal discussion about our core concepts, but over time, as we developed our parenting style, Shaun and I noticed that four ideas started recurring more and more. When we first started parenting, I think we quickly recognized the Be Flexible core concept, but some core concepts took longer to develop or weren't things we settled into until our kids were a little older. I do believe that often parents are naturally creating their core concepts—they just haven't taken the time to sit down and analyze their parenting enough to realize what those are.

How to identify your core concepts:

- Take the time you need to really think about your parenting.
- What are you doing well? What are you not doing well?
- What would you like your children to focus on long-term? For us, it was family and being creators in life in general, which naturally started transitioning into our core value of intentional analog parenting (family time) and our

creator-consumer core value. Others may find core values with a religious focus, an educational focus, or a service-based focus.

Once you have identified your core concepts, think about other ways you can pull those into your parenting. Are there new rules that need to be set so that you can achieve your long-term core value? Is this a core value that needs to transition into your workplace? School? Many of ours transitioned when our kids started school, so we could set and create our family culture to reflect our hopes and expectations.

OUR CORE CONCEPTS

Adapt or Die

"Adapt or Die" is something I always mention to Shaun when it comes to parenting and in areas of our business. You know you are going to mess up in life—and if you can't adapt after you mess up, you're just going to do worse the next time! Sometimes obstacles are put in our way, and we can complain about them or quit, but if we can learn how to adapt, and do it quickly, success can be more easily achieved. This is an important process to teach our children, which will greatly benefit them in the future.

As YouTubers, we learned quickly that we have to make adjustments and be ready to think outside the box every day at work. Success on YouTube requires creative content and favoritism in the platform's algorithm, and every time that algorithm changes, we have to adjust our professional strategy. The faster we can do this, the sooner we can succeed in the new environment. We continually and deliberately reshape what we do in order to meet the needs and expectations of our viewers.

This also helped us become just as digitally savvy as our kids are. We *had* to adapt to the ever-shifting world of social media or we'd never stay on top of a highly competitive business.

We face this "Adapt or Die" philosophy in all areas of our parenting. External influences will always be there. Having our kids learn that they will be able to adapt to a new set of circumstances—such as moving to a new school, trying out a new hobby, running for student body officer, or taking calculus—is a vital life skill. If we allow our kids to be inflexible, the natural give-and-take of daily life will create all kinds of stressors and interpersonal struggles for them. Life doesn't need to be harder than it already is.

When we adopted Daxton, we were not prepared for the immediate shift in our family dynamic. When his struggles with ADHD and autism became overwhelming, figuring out how to best serve his needs while not neglecting our other children became an "Adapt or Die" situation.

At eighteen months, Dax started to manifest neurological differences from our other children at the same age. They showed up in difficult and gut-wrenching ways that forced us as parents to reevaluate our parenting with him. What we had been doing with our other children wasn't working, and at the time he'd not yet gotten a definitive diagnosis. We didn't find a ton of help (yet) in doctors and medicine so we tried to adapt. We shifted our parenting for Dax, making new rules to fit his needs using our "Adapt or Die" core value.

But Dax also taught us that the best-laid plans can be destroyed quickly, too. Normally I'm the mom that likes to have everything in order and organized. With Dax, this just wasn't possible. Meltdowns happened often and without warning. Going out became harder because he wouldn't sit still and found it hard to behave in public. We shifted our parenting to reflect that. Where before I would do the grocery shopping with the kids during the day, now I waited till evening when Shaun was home with the kids. Where before we would attend the kids' school activities as a whole family, now we divided and conquered. I would attend one activity with a child or two and then Shaun would attend the next activity so that we could keep Dax in his comfort zone of home and on his normal schedule. We had to be flexible in order to maintain our own sanity and meet Daxton's need to avoid changes to his routine. I often say that in many ways our family life revolves around Daxton.

This transition took years and in some ways is still ongoing. But during this time we also had to allow for flexibility so that we could still fulfill the needs of our other children. Finding extra room in the schedule for one-on-one time became more important. Instead of sending our kids to their friends' houses, we often encouraged them to have friends come to our house, which allowed us to both interact with them *and* keep Dax on his schedule.

Parenting is difficult in so many ways, and it's a constant process of looking at all the kids and identifying which needs the most urgent attention. Sometimes we did this very well and a few times we didn't. But if you are flexible with your family and yourself, you can find the right balance.

Be Flexible

You'll want your day-to-day house rules for living and expectations to be the exact same for every child. If you have only one child, it is a bit easier to succeed in this, based on their single personality. But if you have more than one child, you'll recognize at some point (probably sooner rather than later) that what works so effortlessly for one child will be a total flop with another. We have some kids we have to essentially force to eat their dinner and others we have to remind not to snack when they're not really hungry. We have a few kids who will easily lay themselves down and go to bed without much reminding, and one that requires extensive monitoring at bedtime. What works for one will not always work for all.

What that actually means, of course, is that flexibility is at the heart of good parenting.

When Dax came along, we were *so* excited to finally have a boy in the house. Shaun had grand plans for football, soccer, and basketball and was already dreaming of the joy he'd feel when our son, the superstar athlete, scored a goal or a touchdown or hit a home run as we happily watched from the bleachers. As soon as Dax turned five, we signed him up for his first soccer team, expecting him to do well. We quickly realized that while he was very fast, he lacked the fine motor skills to know what to do with the ball when he got to it. Instead he would dance around, disrupt the coach's plans, and generally frustrate everyone on the team. After a season or two, we had to admit that team sports were not going to be his strong suit. We could have continued on this path, coaching him, encouraging him, and forcing him to practice until he improved.

It was hard to admit that we'd made assumptions about what our lovely little boy was going to like to do, and what he'd be good at. We had to be flexible or we would have had a miserable child forced into our box of expectations, not his box of strengths. It was an incredibly powerful lesson for us as parents.

So we took a step back, and tried to think about what Dax was showing and telling us about himself with his interests and activities. We noticed that he loved computers and was quickly learning to use them. Not just liking computers as other kids his age did, but wanting to know how they worked and what made a program run.

Once we started to be able to identify our son's natural talent, we adapted. We overhauled our thinking about what we had hoped for him, to be a star athlete, and shifted our own expectations to be on par with who he truly was, and signed him up for a coding class twice a week, an engineering class, and a chess class. What a difference it made! Dax was thrilled, and he was soon coding websites, creating avatars, programming drones, and using his gift to help the technologically slower kids in the class—when he was only seven years old! His success working with computers has built his confidence in a way that sports never could.

YOU ARE EITHER A CREATOR OR A CONSUMER

For me, the perfect day with my kids is a morning spent lazing around the house followed by a family movie, a pizza dinner, playing games, and just hanging out together. On days like that, we are the most contented consumers ever.

With kids, you always want to strike a balance between creating and consuming. Creating doesn't mean you expect an artistic masterpiece—cooking a meal or arranging a bunch of flowers is creating. I have one friend whose daughter started an Instagram account and began to post a lot of selfies. Often the selfies were of her different makeup looks or styles. My friend initially was worried about this account, because her daughter was young, but also seemed a little self-absorbed by posting pics of herself all the time. But soon her daughter's love for her own makeup started to morph into pictures of graphic makeup that a skilled makeup artist would do for a movie. Her daughter talked more and more about makeup and taking classes and really learning the trade. She realized her daughter had a natural gift for makeup and also loved it. This Instagram account became her way to show off her skills and get feedback from other people, and it became a small portfolio of her abilities. She was ten when she started and is now thirteen and an amazing artist with makeup. Had her mom shut down her Instagram account in the moment, she would never have discovered this amazing talent in her daughter.

Over time, we've also been able to help our other kids see that they can create and *make* things happen instead of *waiting* for life to happen. Yes, it's fine to relax and have downtime and aimlessly (or purposefully) surf the Internet or go down the black hole of YouTube watching, but we want our kids to know that most of their time should be spent thinking, and trying, and seeking—and finding ways to contribute to our overall well-being. They know how true this is because they've seen how we took advantage of the opportunity that blogging and YouTube offered us. They know how hard we've worked, and they also know that only in the digital era could I have had the career that brought me and the entire family to such a wide audience. Before the Internet came along, you had to be a professional chef to be on TV and show people how to cook; now anyone can turn on a camera in their kitchen, post a video online, and suddenly have a following.

In this new digital space, we may not always understand how our kids are creating because it sometimes looks a lot like consuming. People still don't fully understand what I do for work. They hear that I create YouTube videos and believe that I halfheartedly turn on the camera and film for ten minutes, and then go about my day. They don't understand the hours of work in creating the ideas and prepping that go into each video, the editing, the post-production, and the uploading using correct SEO, tags, and good description boxes. Nor do they understand that the videos are really just the tip of the iceberg to an entire digital media company that deals with employees, contracts, attorneys, licensing, endorsements, working with Fortune 500 companies, and owning equity in several other companies, which are now a part of what we do.

Consumption can sometimes look a lot like creation, so before assuming your child is only consuming content, you can use this checklist to help identify one from the other:

- Have you had an open conversation with your child about what they are doing and what their interests are? Are they just simply watching cartoons? Or are they studying the graphics, the animation, the color, or the writing of the show? Dax will watch *Apollo 13* thirty times, but every time he is absorbing different information about space, the ship, and the tactics they used to fix the situation. He's watching to learn—not to just simply watch.

- What are your child's long-term goals? Do they have proficiency for that goal? Do they show natural interest in that subject?

- Are they discussing offline what they are also interested in online? Does consumption of material make their minds work and think *after* they have consumed it?

- Is there something tangible at the end? Are they coding a game? Writing a poem? Creating lyrics for a song as they share over the Internet?

- Can you reinforce their interest with analog moments? My friend signed her daughter up for formal makeup classes. They center their gifts for her birthday and Christmas around buying her equipment and tools for her trade.

My YouTube career is a way that I model for my children all the wonderful things that can happen when they are creators rather than just consumers. They've learned, by example, to use their imagination, to think outside the box, and to envision themselves as capable of doing whatever they set their minds to do. This gives them the confidence they need to push past any setbacks and move forward when life isn't fair, safe in the knowledge that I believe in them and will always have their backs.

INTENTIONAL ANALOG PARENTING

Even though we use so much technology and live in such a digital, crazy atmosphere, I think there is a point where you need to have what Shaun and I call *intentional analog parenting*. Regardless of how amazing digital can be, there is nothing that can fully replace real-life, in-person moments. There is a tactile response to things when you do them in real life vs. online. You can't fake family laughter over dinner. You can't smell a flower through a computer screen. The human body has multiple senses and is hardwired for in-person learning. Analog moments allow for that.

This is when you're intentionally giving your children analog moments to keep them well balanced and centered in their otherwise-digital-dominated world. It's actually really easy to do this—just make part of the house rules an analog equivalent for something digital every day. As a bonus, it'll make you feel young again!

For example, get your kids a wind-up alarm clock and have them use that instead of pushing a button on their phone. It's especially handy for those kids who have a hard time waking up in the morning—they'll have to get up to turn off the alarm clock. Or you can have them go on a walk instead of spending all their time on their phones, or weed the garden by hand, or read a real book or magazine instead of one on their devices, or play card games with their favorite physical deck rather than online, or have their friends over and turn the phones off (well, okay, good luck with *that* one!)...remember that while it sounds incredibly obvious to you, one of your jobs as a parent in this digital age is to actively teach your kids how to engage with the real world not through the lens of a screen.

Ideally, you want to find that sweet spot of a balance with analog and digital in everyone's life and as part of the family rules. Too much analog is like sticking your head in the sand, pretending that the digital world doesn't exist—the world is never going back to the way things were when we were young, and in many cases that's a good thing. But too much digital living removes kids from the normal human interactions of face-to-face conversations and hands-on tasks that are still so essential to their growth and maturity. We've found that our kids actually love doing a lot of the analog activities that the digital world has almost rendered obsolete such as playing board games, or building a blanket fort, or going to the lake for a swim. What could be more fun than dinner with the family, camping outside under the stars, or using your imagination?

If you're a parent of teens and this is a new concept, start small. Pick one thing to focus on that's an analog moment. Maybe instead of letting them ride the bus you pick them up from school each day just so you can talk to them. If you are having dinner together, try eating without phones. Take a few extra minutes and encourage a family walk one night a week. What you will find is that removing the digital element forces more interaction. Initially, teens may push back; they will yell and gripe, act angry, and try to make the experience miserable. But if you can push through that, they will eventually realize you aren't going to give up and they will fall in line. After a few months the same teens will likely be the ones reminding you it's time to put your phone down for that walk.

Here's our favorite super-easy trick when we want our kids to have analog time: We turn off the Wi-Fi. It usually takes only a minute or two before every single kid in the house comes out of their room and asks us if the Internet is down. ☺ Instead, they find that we have a planned analog moment!

Chapter 6

Make House Rules, Stick to Them, and Don't Abuse Them

Every family should have rules that work for its household. Ask my kids and they'll roll their eyes as they say, "We have a *ton* of rules." We really don't have a *ton* of rules that aren't just common sense, but structure is good. Systems make us more efficient.

Family rules, as you already know, give structure and boundaries that children crave to make them feel safe. They teach children that they can choose their actions but they can't choose their consequences. Rules work. As long as you remember these three important points:

- Don't make rules you can't or won't enforce. You are not your child's friend. You are the Loving Enforcer!
- Don't make rules you can't keep yourself.
- Don't be so strict about them that your kids burn out and rebel— not because they really want to, but because they feel they have no choice as they can't live up to your strict rules and expectations.

This is especially important as the kids get older. When they're very little, parenting is more about tending to their physical needs; as they grow older, emotional needs become paramount. When there are tough issues, you can go down the rabbit hole really quick, so having rules in place can make things easier for all.

BEHAVIORAL HOUSE RULES

Our behavioral house rules are all designed to focus our kids on their roles as contributors to the family; to strengthen the bonds between all of us; and to ensure that there is total transparency about who is doing what, and why, and what the consequences will be. These rules aren't written into a contract, but my kids know and understand what they are: the way we want them to act, and the way they want to be treated by others. Shaun and I have found that stating these rules regularly is as helpful for the kids as it is for us.

The "Be a Good Person" Rule

These are basics that toddlers can do easily without thinking, so strive to act like this when you're older: Be kind; don't hit or otherwise invade anyone's personal space, but share what you can, when you need to; say you are sorry when you are in the wrong or make a mistake. And most of all, hug often, pray often, do good often, and smile often.

The "Be Honest" Rule

One of the rules my mom had for us as kids—and one that I think is near the top of the list of absolutely essential rules for all families—is the "Be Honest" rule. This is the rule where you tell your children, "If you mess up, I am not going to be mad at you for the mistake. I will always love you, but I will be really mad at you if you don't tell me the truth. So if you're going to mess up, you're going to own up to it and be honest. If you tell me the truth, I promise you I will not get mad at you."

Kids really need to hear this. It's unconditional love stated in a rule that makes them feel that they can confide in you, no matter what, and you will not judge them. You might not be happy about what they did, but you will be happy that they trusted you enough to tell you the truth and face the consequences. I can't stress this enough.

The "Take Care of Our Space" Rule

With six children, we have to be pretty strict about how they treat their environment, and each other in it. This helps all the kids when they end up making a mess (you can guess how often that is!), and will help instill good habits that will be second nature when they have their own homes. This means: No food outside the kitchen; knock on closed doors before entering; turn off lights when you are the last one leaving a room; always flush the toilet, and put the toilet seat down; laundry day is Friday, so if you don't bring your dirty items to the laundry room and sort them, I won't wash them; if you make a mess, you clean it up; keep your room clean and make your bed every day. Also: If you borrow something, return it quickly, and in the same condition and to the same location you found it in.

The "Extra Job" Rule

Guess who hates this rule! I always have a running list of different chores on any given day, and whoever isn't being a team player that day has to do one of them. Often the least favorite job is to make the school lunches for everybody the next day, but I've always got something that I can point to if someone's really not listening. It works especially well when the "Take Care of Our Space" rule is being ignored. Most of the time, I just have to say the two dreaded words—*Extra jobs!*—and my nerves are instantly soothed!

Ideas for extra jobs: clean out refrigerator and wipe shelves, vacuum various areas of house, wipe out and organize kitchen cupboards, weed various areas of yard, organize pantry, wipe and clean out bathroom cabinets, deep clean bathrooms, walk the dogs, vacuum out the car, clean out and organize closets, clean out and sort the attic, dust the house, run extra errands for Mom/Dad, take smaller children on an outing for the afternoon, and so many more.

The "Automatic No" Rule

We've made it clear to the kids that certain things they ask for are going to be subject to the "Automatic No" rule. It's an incredibly handy strategy because it nips things in the bud, and the kids know what they can or can't do or ask for because the answer will automatically be no. So they (usually!) don't bother asking, no feelings get hurt, and this spares you the aggravation of having to be the mean parent who always says no—even if sometimes you actually do want to say yes!

You'll want to create your own "Automatic No" list that works for you. For us, the answer will be no if:

- Mom and Dad don't both say yes. This prevents asking one parent and then asking the other to try to get around the first no, even though the kids will usually still try!
- You ask me in front of your friends to do things. Example … to go over to their house and sleep over. This puts too much pressure on me, as I might not know who the parents are, or where the house is, or what the siblings might be like, or who else is going, so asking in front of friends doesn't give me an opportunity to express and explain my concerns.
- You ask to have your curfew extended without a good reason.
- You ask to borrow my phone because you didn't charge your own.
- You want to do something and your room is a mess. My kids have learned that their room had better be clean before they

even ask, and once I say no, it's not like they can clean it up in a hurry and then ask again. This "Automatic No" works really well except sometimes the kids just...forget!

- You have forgotten something important. You need to be responsible for your work and activities. I'm not going to run it to school for you. If you forget your lunch on the table, it's not going to kill you to go hungry for one afternoon—and it's the fastest way you'll learn to check before you leave the house!

BAILEY, ON HAVING RULES

When we were little, I always wanted to be that kid who didn't have rules at home. We could then do what we wanted, eat what we wanted, go to bed when we wanted, etc. Then we read stories about kids who grew up without structure and rules, having zero accountability, and threw their lives away. They often later talked about how hard it was growing up without a traditional home and structure.

So having rules in your home really helps, because you know what's expected of you. You know what you can or can't do. For example, my sisters and I don't get paid to babysit the little one *unless* I have to turn down a paid babysitting job to stay home. We know one of our family rules is that watching siblings is a responsibility of living in the home.

Some aspects of all these rules make things easier, but now that we're older, I feel like we deserve a little bit more freedom. I know I'm a pretty good kid. I know what

I'm supposed to be doing, and I prioritize my life based on that. I'll know what time I'm supposed to be home, and do my homework, and then go to bed. Yet I might want to go to a friend's house after school, because I know how to budget my time properly. I always have to check in first, and then if I don't hear back from a parent right away, I may get bugged that I've just wasted half an hour that I could have spent with my friend. Even with that, it's still nice to know that my parents care enough about me to give me structure with more freedom as we get older.

The "No Whining That You're Bored" Rule

One of my favorite rules is "No Whining That You're Bored." "Only boring people get bored" is something my kids hear often. They know there is always something to do, to read, to listen to, to watch, or to imagine, and the "No Whining" rule helps my kids manage their time and keep themselves occupied. If they still claim boredom, I happily offer them alternative activities such as cleaning the bathroom, organizing the book closet, or vacuuming the living room. Usually it doesn't take long for them to find something else to do besides whine.

The "Mom Goes to Bed at 9:30" Rule, or Make Sure You Make the Time to Decompress

There's the well-known cliché about the oxygen mask dropping down on the plane and the parent or the adult putting it on first before taking care of the child sitting next to them. Our inborn instinct is to help our children first, but it's also critical to remember that you're not just a parent, you're also a person.

Which means you need to set rules and parameters for yourself, too. When you do, you'll be teaching your kids that *your* rules are in place so that everyone in the family can acknowledge that parents' needs are just as important as kids' needs. In our case, and for any parent who works full- or part-time in the home, as Shaun and I do, we need uninterrupted time to get our work done effectively. One of the rules we have for ourselves is that parental work time means we are off-limits. Just because you're physically in the house doesn't mean you're available to be interrupted (unless, of course, it's an emergency, and your child in hysterics about not finding her cell phone charger is definitely *not* an emergency!).

One of the worst things for a parent is feeling like you're stressed or stretched so thin that you can't relish the simple daily joys around you. Instead it feels like the movie *Groundhog Day* over and over again. Get up, do the kid thing, go to work. Come home, do the kid thing, go to bed. Get up, rinse, and repeat. I'm sure you know what I mean! It's so frustrating when you *want* to spend fun quality time with your kids, but you're so stressed and tired that it automatically becomes cranky time instead of let's-enjoy-our-evening-together time. You just can't do that forever; you're going to be so unhappy and your kids will be, too. You'll feel that they're always pushing your buttons when your stress has risen to catastrophic levels, and then something or someone is going to crash and burn.

I realized how important it was for me to have even a small window of time to tend to my own needs, and do something I love or get my work done, so I set in place the 8 p.m. rule. When the kids were little, we began the bedtime routine at 7:30 so that lights-out was at 8 p.m. No discussion. It was bedtime. Do not disturb Mommy after 8 p.m., unless it's something really important or a valid emergency.

Now that the kids are older, it's the 9:30 rule. As in: Mom goes to bed at 9:30 p.m., then Mindy comes out!

This rule came about because it's so important that kids don't just see parents in the context of what they need, and are aware that their parents are human beings who are entitled to their own space, consideration, and foibles. This is my time to gather my thoughts, and have the time I need with Shaun to interact with him as a couple, not just a strategic parenting team.

By now, the kids are pretty well trained not to bother me after 9:30 p.m., but if the older kids need to ask me a question then, I'm not going to bite their heads off. They know it has to be *really* important. If I don't start to wind down until closer to 11 p.m., this puts me up so late that it's not healthy for me, because I won't be getting enough sleep. My mind has a hard time shutting off at night, going through everyone's schedule for the next day, thinking about video ideas, or how I will manage carpools with my work conference call, and so on. If I can't manage my mind's own restful needs, then Mindy (rather than Mom) will be out not only that night, but into the next day as well!

I get the decompression I need during the evening hours. For others, they might be happy when they can go to a specific kind of club, or join a team or a community league, or spend time volunteering with a local group. Whatever you choose to do, this is time that's all yours.

The "We Will Get to Know Your Friends" Rule

It's very easy to keep tabs on your kids' friends and playmates when they're little, because you need to be supervising, and you'll meet the parents or caregivers of these friends. As your kids get older and their circle of friends widens, you need to keep tabs on who they know—and who they *want* to know (with or without your approval!). This means: I want to get to know your friends, so please bring them to the house; no friends in the house without approval when Mom and Dad aren't home; no opposite gender in the bedroom; I want to meet the parents before letting you go to a friend's house; and we will call to verify parental involvement in all parties you are invited to.

Chapter 7

Becoming the Loving Enforcer and Parenting on the Same Page

Now that you have a good idea of our behavioral house rules, it's time to enforce them. There are two main concepts that have served us well: the Loving Enforcer, and Parenting on the Same Page.

THE LOVING ENFORCER

Becoming the Loving Enforcer is one of the hardest skills to develop as a parent—at least it was for me—and this is a topic that often comes up when we have discussions with other parents online. You don't want to be a helicopter parent, pretending your child is never a problem, or swooping in to instantly rescue them or solve their problems or situations so that they eventually become unable to solve them themselves. You don't want to be the hardliner either, with the "Do it because I said so" kind of stance that some of my friends grew up with, because that is guaranteed to make children frustrated and resentful.

Finding the perfect balance and being a strict but Loving Enforcer comes only with trial and error, and mistakes will doubtless be made.

Shaun and I never see ourselves or define ourselves as our children's "best friends." I mean, are you "best friends" with other children? Of course not! Yes, you absolutely want your children to love you, trust you, and feel that they can confide in you about anything the same way they would with their friends, but you are not one of their peers. You're the parent! This doesn't mean you can't have friend-like moments or enjoy the same things or laugh over funny jokes together. It just means that you always need to remember that you are, in the end, the ultimate responsible party for them. You can be the loving mother or father, but depending on the day, you may also need to be the Loving Enforcer and be able to say no when it makes sense.

A Loving Enforcer is strict but willing to be flexible should the circumstances warrant it (which, I have to admit, doesn't happen a lot in our house!). My children know that I will always love them, but when the rules are broken, the Loving Enforcer unrolls the contract or takes away the phones and the car keys. No amount of begging will make the Loving Enforcer budge one inch. Our kids know that if they make bad choices, there will be definite natural consequences.

Most important of all, a Loving Enforcer is preparing these kids for adult life in the real world, where good people are not always rewarded and bad people sometimes get away with terrible choices. (I'll discuss the notion of what's "fair" on page 181 in Chapter 10.) Life *isn't* fair, which I'll discuss in more detail in the next chapter. So it's up to you as the Loving Enforcer to allow your children to learn that life isn't fair when the prices for their mistakes and the ensuing consequences are low. Family rules need to be followed. At the end of the day, this structure helps make our kids feel safe. Life will be more predictable and that leaves them feeling reassured and loved.

Just this past year, for instance, Rylan just couldn't get herself out of bed, even though we tried to get her up several times. Not surprisingly, the school bus came when she was busy filling up her water bottle. She grabbed it and her backpack and managed to make it onto the bus, but forgot her gym bag with all her volleyball practice attire that she needed in it. The frantic texts soon began to arrive. We could have easily dropped that bag off at school to rescue her, but we would have still had to deal with the consequences of her sleeping in and forgetting stuff for school in the future again. So I just replied, "What a bummer. Sorry, next time hopefully you'll remember." And she will!

These lessons are often harder on the parents than the kids. It's *always* difficult for me when I have to enforce the consequences. Sometimes I feel really awful and question whether I'm being a bad parent. Sometimes you might have other people question your methods, too. Once when one of the twins forgot her lunch, we followed our same rule about not saving her by bringing another lunch to school. We knew she wouldn't starve in the three hours she had left of school, and we also knew she could come home later and eat a snack. But the school informed us that was harsh parenting, fed her a school lunch, and charged it to our lunch account. The lesson for us was that sometimes it can be hard to follow through on consequences when others undermine your parenting. We opted to tell our daughter that she was awfully lucky that someone else took mercy on her that day, but we continued to reiterate that she needed to remember her lunch because that wouldn't always happen.

THE LOVING ENFORCER'S TIME-IN VS. TIME-OUT—FOR THE KIDS AND FOR YOU, TOO!

Time-outs are one of the most common punishments for small children—and they can be just as effective for *you*! Some parents have a time-out corner or chair, where the child has to stay quietly for however long the punishment lasts. Time-ins are the same principle, except the child needs to be near wherever Mom or Dad are for however long you specify.

Time outs or time-ins are the most effective, I've found, when used sparingly. Otherwise, this tool can turn into an easy out for you because it's reactive rather than proactive— the modern equivalent of our parents yelling at us to go to our rooms. Obviously you want whatever's gone wrong to be fixed, but you need to find out what really happened first.

You also need to tailor the time-out or time-in to your kids' personalities. I always do time-ins with Daxton as he can get so physically overwrought, it's better for us both to be in the same place. I'll say something like, "Dax, I'm doing my hair in my bathroom. You can sit right here next to me where I can see you and where you physically have to calm down because I've got my eyes on you." That also keeps him safe and the other kids safe, too.

For the twins, however, a time-in would have been much less effective, because if they were butting heads, it was hard for them to be around each other. I'd send each one off to a different corner and let cooler heads prevail. Inevitably I would know when the time-out was a success because I would soon hear them creeping closer and closer to each other until they would be laughing or chattering in the other room together again.

Sometimes kids can be quite resourceful to get around time-outs. I can remember my mom sending my brother and sister to their rooms only to later find them both lying with their feet in the doorways, but their bodies in the hallway, playing checkers in the middle of the hall. Still technically on time-out, and in their own respective rooms! I can also remember the same siblings driving my brother's remote-control car back and forth between their bedrooms with notes to each other during time-out breaks.

When I get upset, I prefer to have my own time-out someplace where I can take a break if the kids are annoying me and I know I'm about to blow a gasket! It's okay to say, "Mommy needs to calm down. I'm going to my bedroom and I'll be out in ten minutes." Know when your buttons are getting pushed and withdraw—for me, it's the only way to regulate. Because if *you* don't, then the kids escalate behavior, then you escalate behavior, and then a small problem has suddenly started World War III in your living room.

TEST YOURSELF FOR YOUR OWN (BAD) HABITS

How can you be the best possible Loving Enforcer? It starts with you being aware of your own bad habits. Or by admitting that your default response to a certain button being pushed will always be on the wrong side of right. It's just as important for parents to be able to self-correct, learn to apologize, and acknowledge that often we also make mistakes. This shows our kids that it's okay to be human and make mistakes. But that what's most important is learning from them. It also shows kids that parents and children are partners in this journey. We are all trying to figure it out together. If parents can acknowledge their weaknesses, it will be easier for kids to forgive those shortcomings when they are older and admit their own.

The "Put-It-Off" Habit

One of my bad habits that justifiably drives my kids nuts is how I act when I'm super-busy. I'll tell them to do their chores, and then they can come back and ask me if they can go out and do something. They dutifully do the chores, but then I say, "Ask me tomorrow," because I'm preoccupied with something else. I just back-burnered them. They ask me the next day and I say, "Well, let me check my schedule. I'm not sure what's happening," They then ping me several times throughout the day, and I blow up and say, "If you bring it up one more time, I'm just going to say *no!*" The kids know there's always the risk that they're going to annoy me to the point where I'll say no, even if I don't mean to.

One day when I was super-busy with a work project and busily typing away, I heard four-year-old Paisley calling for Mommy through the stairway banister. I had already done the nightly rituals and put her to bed, so I was mildly annoyed to be bothered again. I called out a "Good night, Paisley," and told her to go back to bed. Paisley would not give up, and just kept saying *Mommy*, waiting a few seconds and then calling *Mommy* again. Finally, in my very annoyed Mindy voice, I looked up and snapped, "*What???*" Paisley looked at me with her sad little eyes, tilted her head, and said, "I just wanted to say I love you." *Ugh!!!* A dagger to the heart! Supermom of the year, right there! With six of them around (seven if you count my hubby), an office full of employees, and two dogs, all with individual needs, there's always someone asking me for or about something! This really isn't fair to the kids, and I know that it's my responsibility to make time for everyone—myself, and the people I love.

The "No One Is a Mind Reader" Habit

Another bad habit I think a lot of parents have is forgetting that no one is a mind reader. With schedules shifting so quickly, it's easy to forget as a mom that the rest of the family might not be privy to those changes, but sometimes we still expect the kids to magically know what's expected of them. That's when we slip up and say, "Well, you just should have known," when something goes wrong.

Spell things out clearly. If you're not sure what was said or not, then say it again. Better to get the eye roll, than to be in the wrong!

Also, try paying more attention to the family schedule. Make a calendar and post it in an area where everyone will see it. And be sure to update it regularly!

The "Avoid Admitting You're Wrong" Habit

Even though we all do, no one likes to screw up and admit when they are wrong. Many parents do their best to avoid admitting their mistakes in front of their children. This doesn't make you a weak parent—it makes you a *strong* one when you are able to say, "I'm really sorry, I shouldn't have said that. I blurted it out in the heat of the moment. I didn't mean it." Or, "What can I do to make it better? I'm sorry, I'll try harder not to say or do that again." It makes your kids realize that you have validated their feelings by treating them with honesty and respect, and by being genuinely sorry. This helps them learn how to apologize to their friends when they mess up, too.

It's such an awful feeling when you know you messed up, and you see your child's woebegone facial expression and your heart just sinks.

It's the Bad Parenting Moment we all dread.

Being honest and apologizing might not undo the damage in that moment, but at least your children see you being genuinely contrite. Just know that five years from now when your child gets mad at you for something else entirely, they might still remember your mess-up and give you a verbatim blow-by-blow history of it when you can't even remember what happened! Ha-ha!

All joking aside, I did just do this to my own father not too long ago. We were telling old stories about growing up, and I jokingly brought up a time when I remember my dad having a bad parenting moment. It wasn't a huge deal, and as an adult, I can totally understand why he did it, so I was almost teasing him when I brought it up and retold the story. Later that day my dad pulled me aside and, in all honesty, sat me down to apologize. He felt really, really bad that I had such a memory of him, and expressed his love for me once more. He stated that, in hindsight, he had probably been too hard on me in that moment, and that he wished he could go back and undo that memory. I am so lucky to have such an amazing father, who is not only loving but humble.

Being able to sincerely apologize to our children when we make mistakes is a must. How can we expect them to own up and correct their mistakes if we can't do the same?

PARENTING ON THE SAME PAGE

One of the hardest things for some couples to do is be on the same page about their parenting rules and strategies. This is really crucial if you both want to be the Loving Enforcers with a minimum of triangulation from your children. Shaun and I are very lucky that we both grew up with a strong family structure, have many of the same values and faith, and are able to work out our issues without too much opposition! We've seen too many couples, who appeared to love each other deeply, fall apart and end up divorcing when life became overwhelming and they focused on their differences rather than their strengths.

Shaun: "Here's why parents need rules: I think there's a little bit of a misconception with people about what 'freedom' actually means. Parents who can create a solid framework of rules actually provide themselves some level of predictable outcomes. Those outcomes come with varying degrees of risk and reward. The freedom comes when we choose more and more favorable outcomes, thus gaining trust from within the system. With that trust comes the freedom to switch things up and adapt within the framework, based on a new set of environmental factors. This goes for all aspects of our lives, but becomes especially important once we see what our children's personalities are like and what specific emotional needs they have.

"Rules provide a system within which our children can gain more freedom, primarily as they demonstrate that they are able to make the more favorable choices (from the basics of right and wrong) in a consistent pattern over time."

Giving Each Other Feedback That's Productive, Not Critical

Couples need to get on the same page and spell out their parenting rules, hopefully before they're too deep into a conflict! Because life happens, and there will always be circumstances out of your control—somebody gets sick or your job is eliminated and you have to move, for example—but your rules will go with you wherever you go and whatever you're dealing with.

I know this can be tough, because who's to know which style of rules or parenting ideas are the best. I took the lead on introducing new parenting ideas in our home by researching a lot of books regarding different parenting styles, full of ideas that I wouldn't have thought of on my own. Often, Shaun and I would lie in bed at night and I'd run through thoughts or ideas I had read about. We'd discuss them, and find the basics that fit best for our family. Occasionally, we would hit on something that we just couldn't agree on, and in those circumstances, the only way forward was for someone to give in. That can be difficult, but I feel like we both have given in on things that we felt were important to us over the years, to try to keep it balanced. Parenting between couples is like a successful negotiation; it takes a good middle ground between both parties for things to go smoothly.

It can also be very helpful for parents to write out a contract, or create a rulebook, and revisit it every few months. This is especially useful if you're dealing with unforeseen behavior, as we were with Daxton and his medical situation. If something you thought was set in stone isn't working, ditch it. Be flexible, be honest, and be open to change. That's what we want to teach our kids, right?

Good Cop/Bad Cop and Triangulation

Playing their parents against each other is a skill I think all kids possess! That's where the good cop/bad cop routine can quickly become standard operating procedure if you don't get tough about putting your foot down. Especially when the kids are so sweet and adorable. That said, it can actually be okay to play a role in a certain situation, especially if you and your partner have had a conversation about how you want things to unfold.

One time, when Kamri was little, she forgot her school lunch. She knew the rule. No lunch, too bad, no expecting a rescue. She called me and I told her that we don't drop off forgotten school lunches, and she said, in a quiet, tearful voice, "I know." I told her that I loved her, and she responded with the same, then we hung up. She sounded so sad on the phone, but I knew I had to play Justice on this one. And if this had been a regular occurrence, I would have been, like, "Tough beans, girlfriend!" But Kamri was typically our best child at remembering her stuff and had earned a little more freedom within our family system. She had just forgotten that one day. I quickly called up Daddy on this one, who could come in and play Mercy. Shaun took care of it.

Shaun: "But I did it late. I didn't want to swoop in before she had some cost assessed to her for not having done what she should have, even for something as small as forgetting her lunch. I showed up during her lunch period about ten or fifteen minutes late, with an Arby's sandwich, some fries, and a drink. I remember walking in and Kamri was there sitting in the cafeteria, with her braids and her school uniform, sitting backward on the bench at the lunch table when all the other kids were facing inward talking to each other. She was looking down, swinging her little feet because they didn't touch the floor, and it was heartbreaking. When she finally saw me, she got a big smile on her face, and her friends told her she was so lucky to get to eat fast food when all they had were peanut butter and jelly sandwiches! And she never forgot her lunch again."

Kamri learned her lesson, and Shaun and I caved that day because it was so out of character for her.

So, you can sometimes use the good cop/bad cop scenario to your advantage, but only if the good cop and the bad cop are on the same page. Our kids, for example, know that Shaun is stricter on some things than I am—for example their clothing, how many earrings they can wear, or work-related responsibilities. I'm stricter on how they perform in school, their rooms being clean, and their friends/boyfriends. Kids seem to have a built-in radar for knowing which parent is a pushover about certain issues, so if Mom says no or Dad says no, they go to the other one crying and pleading about what they want. And then if one of the parents caves and is perceived as the good cop just to stop the whining, this can provoke a fight between parents because the bad cop has been undermined.

This is where spelling out rules and having contracts can stave off a lot of the good cop/bad cop potential conflicts, because you can simply point to the rules, and the Automatic No's, and be done with it. Then have a bit of fun and surprise the kids on a day when nothing seems to be going right for them, by bending the rules a little bit and making an exception to them, as we did with Kamri and her forgotten lunch. Sometimes even hard-line cops can be real softies. And the kids will remember what you did long after you did it!

Shaun: "My mom was a very thrifty and health-conscious young mother. We never were allowed to eat sugared cereals. Not only would she sew all our clothes (even our underwear), but she would bake our own bread, give us daily vitamins, and taught us moderation in all things. That often meant sugar. I remember one Saturday, as a teenager, my mom told all four of us kids to get in the car to head into town for a fun day out. We did as we were asked. She took us to a pizza restaurant and told us we could order anything we wanted, even soda. She later took us to an ice cream shop and allowed us to order the Grand Teton Supreme (a monstrous twelve-scoop ice cream banana split). After that, she drove to the nearest candy shop and gave us each $10 to buy whatever candy we wanted. At this point we looked at her suspiciously, asking what was going on, because this was *so* out of character for my mom. She just responded with, 'You kids have been so good lately, I just wanted to do something fun for you that you would never expect!' We were shocked. On the car ride home, we kept waiting for a parental lesson on health and the dangers of gluttony, but it never came. I guess this is why Brooklyn and Bailey like traveling with me now! Moderation in all things, right?" *wink, wink* Thanks, Mom!"

Chapter 8

Being Honest and Safe in a World of Digital Fakery

Growing up in a loving family, engaged in our church and our community in our analog world, meant I felt safe. Safe to run outside and play, safe to attend school without fear of being hurt, and safe at home with my family. But because, as I said earlier, the digital world has expanded our knowledge of current events in a global and instantaneous way, and because society has shifted in ways unimaginable when I was in school—such as needing to have lockdown drills in elementary schools—it seems like we're living in scary times. The best way to make your children feel safe is with age-appropriate honesty, with helping them to discern what's real and what's fake, and by availing yourself of the digital technology, such as phone tracking, that can put everyone's mind at ease.

When they know you are being honest with them, they will be honest with you. I learned a great tip from a friend: She told her children that she would not get mad at them if they did something seriously wrong, *as long as* they told her the truth. That told her children that she trusted them, and by knowing that she wouldn't blow up at them about infractions, they were far less likely to go off the rails. It's important, even with scary stuff or inappropriate behavior, that kids know their parents won't immediately fly off the handle. This becomes even more important when the kids are older and parents too often immediately react in a negative way to being told something. Sometimes kids just want a neutral sounding board, not criticism or intervention, so they can figure out solutions on their own—but if they know they're going to get shut down or yelled at, they're less likely to open up. Be sure to offer different options to kids on what they want to do, with one of them being parent intervention. I try to force my kids to handle their own issues, but I do step in occasionally when I can see it's not working.

BEING HONEST ABOUT THE TOUGH STUFF

When I was growing up, my parents weren't super open about difficult subjects because they didn't know how to broach them, or were themselves embarrassed by those subjects. I feel a lot of parents are like this, choosing instead to assume their kids will learn about difficult subjects from school, friends, or books/TV, etc. When I became a parent I made a concerted effort to ensure my kids heard about the tough stuff from me first. I wanted to have open communication on difficult subjects and allow my kids to ask me questions before the world got to them.

Open Lines of Communication

Your kids might have zero interest in porn, drugs, or drinking, but I can *guarantee* that some of their peers do. Your child is going to have friends whose parents have different rules, and might be much more or much less strict that you are. Let's say your son is at a friend's house, and the friend's older brother comes home with some of his friends, and they start showing everyone what's on their phones, including images that are graphic and upsetting or that involve bullying or sexting. What can you do about that?

In order for your kids to be prepared to govern themselves, they have to be informed. I cannot overstress the importance of having open and honest conversations with your kids and teaching them your thoughts and feelings on difficult subjects before the world does. You can have age-appropriate conversations, but they still need to be happening. We don't shy away from any topics that naturally come up in our house. We use correct anatomical terms for our body parts and teach even our little kids that there is no more shame in using the words "penis" and "vagina" than in saying "elbow" or "nose." All of my children have had many conversations about puberty and what it means and looks like well before the school ever did their maturation programs. Now that I have older teens, we've had conversations about STDs, vaping, sexting, pornography, the underage sex trade, etc.

I'm actively having those really sensitive conversations with my kids from twelve years old and up. This may sound young to some parents, and it's always within your prerogative to decide when these conversations happen, but I wanted to be the first relayer of information to my kids. I didn't want the Internet, social media, or their friends to teach them before I did, and I realize that with digital media, it happens much younger than some of us imagine.

This is where the "Teach and Govern" principles, which I discuss in Chapter 10, can be your fallback. As you know, your role as a parent is to teach your children correct principles and let them make decisions accordingly. When they're confronted with options, it's up to *them* to make good choices or bad choices. In the example above, your son might ignore the older brother or leave. He might tell his friend that he won't be coming back if the brother is going to act like that. Or he might eagerly watch what is on the brother's phone. But because you've taught your son to have good character, even if he makes a bad choice, he'll realize that what he did was wrong. He'll turn a bad choice into a good lesson on his own because you've taught him how to govern himself.

We teach our kids to use the "I'm not feeling well" excuse when they are in a bad situation and need us. Our kids can, at any time, tell their friends they aren't feeling well, excuse themselves to a bathroom, call one of us and ask to be picked up right away, and we will drop everything to go get them. No questions asked. It gives them a safe and easy way to save face in front of their friends while still removing themselves from the situation.

We have also used a "safe" word before. Perhaps the word is "elephant" and your kids are in a situation where they can excuse themselves away from their friends. This is when they can text us and say something like, "Mom, you know I love elephants." This is my clue to call my kids and suddenly have an urgent situation at home they must be back for. I've also seen parents who have a specific safe letter or symbol, and if that appears in a text from their kids, that means the parent should call or come immediately.

Our kids know that Shaun and I are invested in their well-being and check on them not to snoop and be intrusive, but instead to make sure they are okay. I firmly believe that most kids choose to do what's right. I wonder if kids who act out and those who have serious issues sometimes aren't held accountable for their behavior by their parents. Kids like this are begging for boundaries and rules that make them feel safe and cared for.

That's why it's so important to be preemptive. Your kids need to be afraid that you might find out something and to know that you mean business when it comes to consequences. When you enforce the rules lovingly but without exceptions, they'll feel safer and behave in a way that will make you proud. Shaun and I always check up on parties before we take our kids to them, making sure parents will be home and that supervision will be happening. We need to have basic information such as location, time they will be home, whether they'll be going anywhere else, etc., and they must let us know if the plans change for any reason.

If you asked my kids what would happen if they broke a rule, they'd tell you, "My mom would find out. She would definitely find out. *Somehow*, she would always know!" I guess this is the digital equivalent of having eyes in the back of your head!

Your intent isn't to terrify your children into obedience. Rather, you want to let them know that you are smart about social media and well connected to other parents, and that you'll use this knowledge and these connections to figure out what they're trying to get away with. Don't moms always know?

The Truth Squad

It's never easy to pick up the phone and share information with other parents about their own children, but this is something I've done many times—my friends and I jokingly call it the Truth Squad. There is enough trust between us and the parents of our children's close friends that we're all able to reveal sometimes-difficult information about each other's children in an attempt to make the collective whole stronger. This is why, as I've mentioned previously, it's so important to have a circle of trusted parents who share similar values and goals and have similar rules. With social media ruling so many aspects of our children's lives, it really does take a village to raise a child.

When dealing with kids, information is power. When I do feel the need to talk to other parents, I do so without any judgment. I know it could just as easily be me getting an awkward phone call from another mom or dad. In fact, next time it probably will be me as it has in the past! We always tell the kids that they can choose their actions but *not* the consequences of those actions.

Trust me—this works! As long as you are consistent and stick to your role as the Loving Enforcer.

Let me share one example: Just this past year, my girls were telling me that vaping (smoking with a small electric device that distributes nicotine via flavored water vapor, rather than smoke from cigarettes) was becoming a trend among teenagers at their school. I assume these kids believed that vaping would be a risk-free buzz because they weren't actually inhaling tobacco smoke and wouldn't get lung cancer. It isn't—vapors are exposed to toxic chemicals, and nicotine is still a highly addictive and dangerous substance.

One of the twins also mentioned that her friend—let's call her Stephanie—had begun vaping a few weeks before and was strategically hiding the habit from her parents.

As part of the Truth Squad, I knew that I needed to inform Stephanie's mother of what was going on. Trust me, it was an awkward call to make, but I knew that it's what I would have wanted if the roles had been reversed.

When I did call her, I told her what I knew in generalities. I pointed out that, since it was hearsay, it would be best to observe Stephanie's behavior before approaching her about it. I also told her how much I appreciated her friendship and that if she found out from Stephanie that my girls were involved, too, I would like to know.

A few days later, I received a call from Stephanie's mother thanking me for the tip. She and her husband had noticed that Stephanie ran to the shower whenever she returned home. When they tried to have a casual conversation, she dashed up to her room with some excuse, promising to talk later. They realized that, if Stephanie was vaping, showering would be a good way to hide the smell. Her behavior was odd enough for her parents to grow more concerned, and they decided to search her things. They found a vape device hidden in her car.

As I mentioned previously, the Truth Squad goes both ways. It's easy to point out the flaws in other people's kids, but it's not so easy to hear it back about our own kids. We always want to believe that it isn't our kids who are up to no good, but we have to fight the natural impulse to think that way and accept that the truth almost always lies in the middle.

When the twins were in third grade, another mother in my Truth Squad told me that her daughter said Brooklyn had slapped another girl in the face during lunch. My first reaction was to say, "Not *my* Brooklyn! She's never hit anyone!" Even at that age, Brooklyn was the most motherly of all my children, so I couldn't believe what I was hearing. Nonetheless, I resisted the Mama Bear impulse, thanked the other girl's mother, and said I would talk with Brooklyn when she got home from school.

I met the twins at the door after they'd got off the bus. By this point, Brooklyn knew that *I* knew what had happened, and she immediately burst into tears. Both she and Bailey began to recount the incident. The other girl had found out which boy Brooklyn liked. She teased Brooklyn for several minutes, shouting the boy's name loud enough for everyone to hear. Brooklyn, who is very reserved, became frustrated. The girl started to taunt Brooklyn, saying that she was going to tell the boy that Brooklyn wanted to marry him, and she started up from the table and headed in the boy's direction. Brooklyn's frustration then boiled over, and my daughter slapped the other girl in the face.

Was it mean for the other girl to incessantly tease Brooklyn? Yes. But Brooklyn's use of physical violence in response was much worse. It's far easier to deflect words than a fist. Shaun and I figured out an appropriate punishment, which included apologizing to the girl, and we also had a discussion with Brooklyn about what to do in situations like this in the future.

Since we can't physically be everywhere, the Truth Squad allows us to be more effective parents to our children as a collective whole, but only as long as it is not abused. Hopefully, your Truth Squad of trusted friends and other parents will enable you to share information that *should* be shared when children are breaking rules or acting out in ways that are harmful. It takes a village to help keep our kids safe.

One of the good things about the digital age is there is so much information we can share via the digital world! If you are a working mom, rely on other moms at work to share and swap information about new apps or things kids are facing. Staying current online with your digital friends can also allow parents an easy touch point to new information. I have a group of women that I reach out to sometimes with questions like "I'm experiencing [...] with my child. Have any of you seen this, and if so, how did you work through it?" I also participate in an online forum for moms of autistic kids located in and near Dallas. I've never met any of these women in real life, but I've used so much information from this group. New tactics to try, the best local doctors or therapy centers for autistic kids, stores or event centers that cater to autism, or even just a listening ear for the days we need to rant to other moms who might understand what we are going through.

Phone Tracking

While the outside world might be a safer place today than it was thirty years ago, we can also use our kids' phones to track their movements. Tracking was impossible when we were growing up, but I don't think our parents worried as much about what we were doing after school because there was no virtual world to intrude on our real world, and we were never that far from home. Though it might sound intrusive, tracking actually allows kids the freedom to go where they like without parents being overly concerned. Part of growing up is breaking rules and having to deal with the consequences, but because Shaun and I can keep a closer eye on our kids' movements than our parents could on our own, those consequences are guaranteed to be a little bit more manageable.

Always Be Honest About Tracking

Whenever possible, I believe you should give your kids the exact same controls on your devices that you put on theirs. I can track their phones—and *they* can track *mine*. It's only fair, although sometimes this drives me crazy. I'll get messages like, "Mom, you went to the movie without us?" or, "Mom, we see you at BJ's, bring us home a pizookie." Nevertheless, tracking me makes *them* feel safe, and that makes *me* feel safe, too.

If you do plan to make phone tracking a house rule, be up-front about it. Children deserve to know when we're keeping an eye on them. Otherwise, we'd be spying and invading their privacy, and we'd cross the line from concerned parent to unethical authoritarian and damage our kids' trust in us. I would think of doing this only if I suspected my kids were in trouble or doing something illegal that would endanger their lives.

As specified in the family cell phone contract, we can check each other's texts, and text threads can never be deleted before Shaun or I see them. We don't text anyone inappropriately, so if the kids want to read anything we write, it's fine. (Believe me, they don't, because my texts are so *boring* to them!) We all want to help each other communicate, stay in touch, and feel safe.

Tips and Tricks

- I can't tell you how many times we've been able to find a misplaced cell phone just by having the tracking via "find friends" and "find iPhone" software enabled on all our phones!

- There are also apps that allow parents to track kids' cars, some even by your car's automobile manufacturer. These apps will show you where your teens have been, where they are currently, how fast they were driving, or even if they go outside a set driving radius you established. I don't really use these, as I have found my phone tracking to be enough, but these are certainly options for parents who want that information.

BROOKLYN'S TEEN PERSPECTIVE ON PARENTS READING TEXTS AND TRACKING THEIR KIDS, AND TRUST (OR LACK THEREOF!)

I don't like phone tracking; even though I'm a good kid and I know I'm never going to do anything wrong, it's felt like my parents didn't trust me. I also disliked that they felt that they had the right to read my messages—it gives them access to all of this information on me and I have no privacy at all. It wasn't that I was saying anything to hide; I just didn't like the feeling of not being trusted. Nobody likes their stuff being pried through—even if you're only scrolling through Instagram, nobody enjoys it if someone is peering over your shoulder.

Texting is basically the only way we communicate anymore unless it's in person. So for me, having your texts read is like the digital equivalent of having your diary read. Also that it's random, so you never know if something private you shared was read by your parents or not. Sometimes it was like you were texting your best friend about this boy that you might have liked, and all of a sudden you walk into the kitchen and your mom is, like, 'Oh my gosh, who's this John kid?' And you've never told her about John—she just read your messages. That's the kind of stuff that bothers me.

I also want to know that there's one part of my life that's only mine. You own your ability to communicate and understand why the rules are in place, but it doesn't mean you're not going to chafe. Being tracked really bothered me when I was in a relationship and I felt like that was stuff that you and that person share, and even though we never did anything that I needed to hide, even texting I love you, have a good night, felt so uncomfortable when I knew someone else could be reading that. And that someone else might be thinking and reading and judging how you're acting and what you're saying—and especially, judging it in a way that you don't think is fair. It's not what *you* meant but they're filtering it through their adult perception. You want to be allowed to make your own mistakes.

I appreciate Brooklyn's opinions and openness here. She has the right to feel this way and has the right to her informed opinion. I think that some adults may even agree with her and feel that reading their teen's texts can be an invasion of privacy.

I mean, I get it. But you wouldn't hand the keys to your car to a fifteen-year-old without them first passing driver's education and countless parent-in-car driving hours. A cell phone or a computer offers a huge degree of accessibility, much like a vehicle does, with dangers at times that even the most experienced users will not be able to avoid.

I think my best practices recommendation on this is to be strategic about what you're looking at. It's important to acknowledge the right to privacy that everyone in the family has, and to be clear about what everyone can but also can't do. I try not to infringe upon my kids' privacy when I don't need to, but I do randomly spot-check things. We have done deeper dives into reading text logs only in instances where we felt that something was being hidden from us, and this has come in helpful as mentioned earlier about me taking Brooklyn's phone away after seeing angry retaliatory texts sent to her ex after a breakup, or when we caught Rylan bullying a friend via text. We delve in only when there is irrefutable evidence that they broke the rules. I want my kids to know that I respect them and trust them until I can't. But when I need to, I gently remind our teens that they are more than welcome to buy their own phones and set up their own cell phone plans if they want. None of the kids has ever taken us up on this offer.

The goal is that by the time our children are eighteen, when they leave home for college, they are educated and prepared to monitor and protect themselves from any potential online intrusions, just like how we prep our teens to drive a car by taking driver's education and proving their knowledge in passing the driver's exam. It is to help them know how to handle or avoid future pitfalls they encounter on the road.

WE NEED TO TALK ABOUT SEXTING

One of the most important reasons for keeping tabs on your kids' phones is due to sexting. This is when sexual images—whether real (of the person sending it) or fake (the person sending it is using someone else's images)—are sent via text or posted on social media. I wish I could say this was an isolated phenomenon, but it isn't. If your kids are honest about what they've seen, and what their "nice" friends are sending to each other, you might be shocked.

I have three pieces of advice about sexting:

1. Have open conversations with your kids! I know I'm repeating myself, but I can't overstress this enough. Talk to your children about what sexting is. Use graphic, detailed language, not general foggy terms. Let them know that this will happen at some point. That they will feel pressure to either request or send photos that aren't appropriate. Talk to them in detail about what it means to pass along underage pornography and the serious consequences it can bring. Use examples! When we see stories on the news about other children getting caught up in passing along pornography and getting in trouble, we

talk to our kids about it. We direct-message (a great digital advantage) the articles off Facebook or Instagram right to their phones and then follow up with conversation at home about what they thought. Ask questions they can't answer with a simple yes or no. Instead of asking, "Do you see sexting happening at school?" ask, "What are some examples you have seen at school that involve sexting?" This forces them to open up and share.

2. Start teaching correct behavior. Teach both boys and girls that it isn't okay to request sexting photos. Teach them not to send them even in jest. There is a big need in general for parents to step up teaching correct social behavior online. We spend a lot of time teaching social behavior in real life analog moments, but forget to also talk about what that looks like online. Teach both boys and girls how to say *no* and to stand up for each other when they see other kids saying no.

3. Don't overreact. I can remember one time when Bailey received an unsolicited photo from someone that revealed a man's penis. She was young and wasn't totally sure what the close-up picture was exactly, so she came to me and said, "Mom, what is this?" I think she suspected what it was, but was so caught off-guard she wanted to alert me immediately. I looked at it and said, "A penis and testicles." I could tell she was horrified and it actually made the situation easier for me not to freak out over. Instead I sat down and we talked about how, yes, that's what a man's body parts look like, but no, she should not have received that. We talked about where it came from, how to avoid this in the future, why it's not okay to send pictures like that, and what to do if she received them ever again. Then Shaun and I spent time figuring out why she had been able to get that picture in the first place and fixed that

issue. (We reported this instance to the local FBI since Bailey was a minor at the time the image was received.)

If I had yelled at her or freaked out, it wouldn't have helped the situation and might have made her feel even more uncomfortable and awkward. In the end we had a nice convo about a tough topic. If she had felt me tensing up, she also would have, and the lines of communication would have shut down between us. Keep your cool and they will see that these conversations aren't strange or awkward.

BROOKLYN, ON SEXTING AND SEARCHES

No Sexting!

A couple of years ago, I liked this boy and we were talking, and his friend sent me a picture of my crush naked but they'd put emojis over his private parts. They thought it was hilarious but I was horrified! I freaked out and handed the phone to my mom. If he'd sent that photo to somebody else who thought it was funny and then *they* sent it to somebody else... it could have ended up all over the Internet. Kids have even been arrested for forwarding along naked photos of other teens. Don't do it!

Searches Can Lead You...

When I was in fourth grade, I had to do a school project and needed a photo of a family holding hands. I went to Google images and typed that in the search bar, and the first three links that popped up were *horrible*. It was my first experience with something like that, and I slammed my computer shut, and I was, like, oh my gosh, what did I just see? You can't un-see it. That's when I realized that something as simple as a search on a completely innocent topic can lead to a problem. There's no way of knowing what's out there, so we must always be careful.

DISCERNING WHAT IS FAKE OR NOT IN THE DIGITAL WORLD

Social media has made it so easy to fake it!

There's perception (aka Pinterest), and there's reality (an unfiltered photo of what your family *really* looks like, before or after that seemingly perfect shot—you know, when someone was crying, someone was yelling, and someone was sulking!). We call it the Pinterest Phenomenon. You've gone through it every time a friend or stranger posts something amazing, and you think, *Wow, that mom sure has it going on! What's her secret? How come her birthday cake has three gorgeous layers and perfectly piped icing flowers when my sheet cake came from a mix and got a little burnt around the edges?* But, of course, you don't know what that mom had to do to get that fabulous shot. Maybe she took a cupcake decorating class, or maybe—just maybe!—she bought that cake at a bakery and passed it off as her own because she had a really bad day at work and didn't have time to make one. Even further out there, maybe she has a maid, a nanny, or a cook, who did all the work and she simply showed up to take the photo.

It's not just the images that are fake, of course. It's seeing what your friends post and how their life looks so wonderful, and then you feel like you're doing something wrong because you can't keep up or things are particularly tough at the moment. Screaming kids, messy house, forgotten carpools—you know what I mean. But the truth is that you can't ever know what the backstory is with those Internet Wonder Women unless you witness it yourself or they tell you personally.

With the Pinterest Phenomenon, it is important to understand that you are only seeing a tiny sliver of what likely took place due to a highly edited, wonderfully staged, perfectly lit photo or video. You aren't easily able to see that person's similar life struggles in the moments right before, or after, that person took the photo or video. The lesson here is not to take what you see online at face value.

The saying I grew up with is: The grass is greener where you water it. In other words, where you put your time and energy leads to whatever is going to grow and develop. If you're always thinking about how other people's grass is greener, or more perfectly manicured, or the size of their lawn is bigger than yours...your own grass is going to die.

So don't fall for the fake and don't fall into the comparison trap. Water your own grass, and your lawn will thrive!

HOW CAN YOU TELL IF SOMETHING IS FAKE?

How can you tell if what you're seeing is scripted or real? Do you remember when *America's Funniest Home Videos* first went on the air? The videos were adorable, and hilarious, and totally real. Once viewers realized how much prize money they could win, however, the videos went from cute and unpredictable to staged, phony, and not so funny anymore.

This has morphed into the "It's Gotta Go Viral" phenomenon. Some viral videos are incredibly hilarious or heartwarming, and totally unscripted. Others are so fake and predictable that you have to wonder why you wasted any time watching them!

More important, our kids are amazingly adept at Photoshopping their selfies, and their friends are, too. Talking about this over and over again with your kids is necessary in the digital world. You have to emphasize many times and in multiple ways that what they see online isn't real life.

In general, I tell my kids to assume anything that comes out of TV or a magazine is edited. Clearly the photographs or TV footage are edited and morphed for maximum appeal. Online it can be harder to identify. Sometimes you can spot a distorted line or weird pixilation, but apps are so advanced now that you can literally edit almost every photo you post in a matter of minutes if you want to.

A good rule of thumb is that if it looks too good to be true, it probably is. I try to teach my kids to be content posting images that are authentic and real, but I also know that occasionally I get a nice shot of myself that I also clean up a little by removing a bad zit or lightening a little under my tired mom eyes. I don't think it's a big problem as long as my kids aren't obsessing over every photo and image of themselves. Yet again, conversation is key. Constantly reaffirming your love for them no matter what they look like and constantly reminding them that photos can be faked are musts.

For example, I had an Instagram friend who took a picture of a beautiful stack of pancakes that would make any foodie drool. A few hours later, she posted the zoomed-out original of the same picture that included the same yummy pancakes sitting on the table, but also included her in her pajamas with splotches of pancake batter all over them, a disaster in the kitchen, and a crying baby screaming while dumping food on the floor. All of us can take events in our lives, zoom them in, add a filter, crop, or Photoshop the image to make it look like a picture-perfect moment, when in reality it wasn't. Kids need to learn this at a young age so they can decipher what's fiction and reality, and learn not to feel competitive with the imaginary world they are seeing online. That goes for fake friends, too, as Bailey explains in the sidebar here.

BAILEY, ON "FAKE FRIENDS"

Brooklyn and I are pretty good at figuring out who's a fake friend, and we can usually sniff those people out fairly fast. You learn how to recognize certain characteristics—you know your genuine friends are interested in how you are doing, and what you are up to, but they don't incessantly ask about it all the time. They just get excited when you tell them any details, and then they support you in everything that you do. They show up to your concerts and performances. But they're not asking, "Hey, can we take a picture together and tag me in it, okay?" so they can gain more followers. They aren't only acting interested in your life when they suddenly need something from you, or a social push. We've had students in our school who feel they are too good to hang out with us, until their thirteen-year-old cousin hears that they go to school with us. The next day, they act like our best friend as they ask for an autograph or quick video saying hi for their cousin. We don't mind doing that at all, but it sure shows who your real friends are. There's just a way that people go about their conversations with you that makes it obvious whether or not what you do professionally online is all they care about.

PAY ATTENTION TO CATFISHING

Shaun: "Another word to add to your digital vocabulary is 'catfishing.' This is when someone creates a fake profile online in order to hide his or her true identity and trick people, for whatever reason. We had a scary experience with what we thought was someone trying to catfish Kamri, and it's worth sharing this as a cautionary tale.

"Kamri has a large social media following of her own, and recently another teen influencer who's very well known followed Kamri on one of her social media accounts. (I'll call the other teen Lisa, which isn't her real name.) They're about the same age, and communicated via direct messenger, and then Lisa said, 'Hey, follow me over on my personal Snapchat,' which Kamri was eager to do. They talked back and forth for several months, and developed a nice friendship.

"Mindy and I were a bit skeptical when they first became friends. We knew it looked like the real Lisa was sending all these messages, but it could easily have been an imposter. Although we're influencers and we have quite a wide reach, there was still a pretty big lack of parity between Lisa and my daughter; Lisa had a lot more influence in the industry and Hollywood. So when Lisa asked Kamri how to use a PayPal account, Kamri started to get worried. She came to us for advice, and I told Kamri what to ask; Lisa explained that when the account was set up, she apparently got locked out, and now in order to get logged back in, she needed her bank account and routing numbers. She claimed her parents didn't know how to use her PayPal account, so she just needed to know how to access it so she could donate to a charity and was thus asking Kamri questions.

"At this point, my radar was on red alert. I was thinking there's still a chance that this is really Lisa and really her large Instagram account. She had already DM'd Kamri from there to send her to her private Snapchat account, but now the conversation was going into an area that sounded really fishy. Why would someone of her caliber, who would have managers, agents, parents, and all these people involved in running the business side of her career, need help with her PayPal account from my daughter? I told Kamri I thought this could be a catfishing situation, and that the real Lisa might have been hacked, or was an imposter all along. (Sometimes, catfishers pretend to be a real celebrity or influencer by changing one letter of that person's name, such as a small *l* to a capital *I*—something you should always be aware of.)

"Kamri, of course, had been having a relationship online with Lisa for several months at this point, felt like she trusted her, and wanted to help her. I was worried that if this was a catfisher, that Kamri might inadvertently give private info in the process and would wake up to find her own bank account drained. So I told her, 'Well, why don't you go back on that original social media platform and direct-message Lisa and screenshot the messages you'd received about PayPal, and ask is this really you or is somebody pretending to be you?'

"Fortunately, in the Instagram platform, Lisa wrote back and said, 'Yes, it's me.' Kamri then told her what my red flags were, and that if she had a question, to talk to *her* dad, and if not, she could call me and I would be happy to walk her through it. Through that process we figured out that Lisa had her own PayPal account because her managers and parents were smart enough not to give her access to other types of bank accounts. She often made money on Live.ly, which was a sister platform to Musical.ly, where you could make money from people sending you gifts (basically points). You could convert those points to PayPal dollars through your Live.ly account, and Lisa wanted to donate hers to a dog shelter, Paws. She *was* genuinely asking Kamri for help. It was such a relief, and when Kamri explained why I was so worried, Lisa was deeply apologetic, and grateful that we were trying to protect her. We all know how much hacking is going on. And even though I didn't know Lisa personally, I'm a parent and I would want to treat her the way I would my own daughter.

"This was an excellent lesson not just for Kamri (and Lisa) about how skeptical they need to be about the trolls, bots, hackers, catfishers, and scam artists lurking online. And it was extremely gratifying that Kamri came to me right away for help. All our kids have seen us manage our social media presence, with all the good and bad that comes with it, and Kamri's initial reaction was, 'I'm not sure how to help; I'd better ask my dad.'

"For all situations where kids aren't sure what to do, especially if they're being catfished, having the default response be 'I'm not sure how to help; I need to speak to my parents' is the way to go. It's not so much about the particular situation, but about teaching your children how to judge situations and when to go to an adult when they realize it's something they can't (or shouldn't) manage on their own."

CAR SAFETY

Although driving isn't digital (yet!), one of the biggest worries we have is when drivers spend more time looking at their phones than at the road. Texting while driving causes crashes, especially with teenagers who are addicted to their phones. So in the interest of covering all the bases regarding digital safety, I think it's important to have a conversation about driving.

Good driving is one of the most important skills your teens can have, and with all the distractions of cell phones now—which didn't exist when Shaun and I were learning to drive—it's more crucial than ever to spell out expectations to ensure not only that the rules of the road are followed but that your kids stay safe. Cars are a necessity in communities without public transportation, and taking away driving privileges can be as devastating (and problematic) as taking away cell phones. When your kids know that these rules will be strictly enforced, it's easier for them to have their friends behave responsibly when driving or as passengers, too.

Also, each point in the contract is meant to open up a bigger convo between kids and parents so they can discuss their feelings in person. This is especially important when you're discussing drinking and driving.

THE MCKNIGHT FAMILY CAR CONTRACT

The following contract between _____ and _____ seeks to establish family rules and consequences regarding car usage.

CHILD REQUIREMENTS

____ I agree that I will always wear my seat belt when I am in *any* motorized vehicle. I agree that I will always insist that any passengers will also wear their seat belts.

____ I agree to ride only in vehicles with the same number of seat belts as passengers. I further agree that I will not transport more people than my car has seat belts.

____ I agree to abide by any state laws regarding my age and driving. (Example: If the state mandates that I have only one passenger from ages sixteen to eighteen, I will abide by that rule.)

____ I will not text or talk on my cell phone while driving. If a call is urgent, I will pull over and then talk.

____ I acknowledge that my parents can install apps that prevent my phone from working or texting while I am driving.

____ I understand that my parents can use apps or other tracking software to track my car, my driving, and my phone.

____ I will always have my driver's license and insurance in the car while I am driving. I will ensure that both are current and not expired.

____ I agree to maintain active car insurance that fits any requirements by my car loan and protects me, my family, and any other drivers adequately.

____ I will regularly check my oil, change wiper blades, and maintain proper tire pressure. I will work with my parents to quickly resolve any car maintenance issues that might pop up.

____ I will ensure that my car stays clean and regularly remove items that don't belong, trash, or other junk. I will vacuum my car once a quarter. I will keep air fresheners in the car to ensure that it has a nice smell.

____ I will not smoke, vape, or carry/do drugs in my car. I will not allow others to do this either.

____ I will never give my friends permission to drive my vehicle without my parents' approval.

____ I will obey all road rules and signs. I will not drive in a reckless manner. I will not speed.

____ I will not pick up strangers or give rides to friends of friends that I don't know.

____ I will be aware of where I am parking and my safety when walking to my car at night. I will ask for someone to walk me to my car if I feel unsafe.

____ I will *not* drink and drive. I will always call a parent, a friend, or a ride service.

____ I will not ride in a vehicle with others that are intoxicated.

____ I will always call for a ride even if I get in trouble for being exposed to substances.

____ I will not park in tiny spaces where it is likely my car will get door dings. Rather, I will park farther out and walk a little more. Exercise is good for me.

_____ If I am in an accident, I will immediately call police and parents. I will not leave the scene of the accident!

_____ I will take photos of both cars if in an accident, including the license plate of the other car. I will ask for insurance info from the other driver. I will provide my insurance to them in the form of my name (first only), my parents' names, my parents' cell numbers, and my insurance company and policy number. This will be written on a separate piece of paper. I will *not* allow them to take a picture of my insurance card, as it has my personal address on it.

_____ I will ensure that my gas tank is at least a quarter full at all times. A quarter tank is the new empty.

_____ I will do a lap around my car before getting into it to ensure that it is in a safe condition to drive—checking tires, looking for fluid leaks, etc.

_____ I will always keep a safety kit inside my car—first aid kit and spare tire, jumper cables, air pump, etc.

_____ I will keep my keys in a safe place at all times to avoid getting them lost or stolen. I will keep a spare set of keys in my home with my parents.

_____ I will keep my music at a safe volume so that I can hear warning sounds, like sirens and honking, etc.

_____ I will not use my vehicle to drive to places that I did not disclose to my parents.

_____ I will follow all safety protocols such as using turn signals, obeying street signs, etc.

_____ I will never be negative or talk back to a police officer, should I ever be pulled over. I will provide all requested information expeditiously, and in a kind manner.

PARENT RESPONSIBILITIES

____ I will provide a working, reliable vehicle for my child.

____ I will teach by example and follow the above rules myself.

____ I will not overreact if my child makes honest mistakes, but rather use them as teaching opportunities.

____ I will teach my child how to maintain their car and how to handle emergency situations like flat tires, an empty gas tank, etc.

_____ _____

(Child's Signature)   (Date)

_____ _____

(Parent's Signature)   (Date)

_____ _____

(Parent's Signature)   (Date)

Chapter 9

The Family Responsibilities

The best way I know how to get my kids to put their best face forward is to make sure that I'm helping them develop as analog people, not just Digital Natives. Here is why chores around the house make them more responsible; here is how we make sure we get what we want and need from the kids in exchange for their getting what they want from us (which is very often something on the digital spectrum); here is how we raise them to understand that their actions have consequences that affect the whole family, whether that's playing music too loudly and disturbing others, or accidentally exposing the family network to a virus by downloading something they shouldn't.

We always say that our home is a micro-economy, and we run it like that. Everyone has jobs, everyone participates in our little society, and then our little society functions properly. It's not that one person is doing everything and another one is not. We're always striving to find that balance.

One of the biggest questions our kids will ask is, "Why do I have to do this and you don't?" You can't just say, "Because I'm the mom," or the dreaded "Because I said so." Kids deserve the respect of a proper response even when they ask a question you might not want to answer! Being able to fall back on your rules will usually help you get through this. And one of the rules we define super-clearly is about chores.

THE CHORE BEAST: KIDS NEED CHORES, AND YOU NEED TO DOLE THEM OUT

As we touched upon in Chapter 6, every child needs the responsibility of doing chores. They teach kids life skills and time management. They teach kids how important it is to help around the house; this goes for boys and girls equally. They teach kids the home hygiene skills they'll need when they're older and living on their own. And they teach kids that they are part of a little society and everyone has an important part in it.

Figure out what works best for your family. Some kids are better on dishwasher duty and others are better helping put the babies down. Chores can rotate through the children by the day, or week, and can change as the kids get older. We tried to mix it up a few times each year. Last year, for example, I had only one kid doing lunches every day as her chore, but it got to the point where she got burned out and the lunches became less and less appetizing. I wised up, and now everyone has to make lunches one night of the week—three nights for Brooklyn, Bailey, and Kamri, and two nights for Shaun and me. Rylan doesn't have a lunch night yet, so she's on dishwasher duty while Daxton is on garbage duty. Paisley is about to join the ritual this year. Everyone has a duty to keep the house clean; the chores mentioned above are more like "jobs."

Do your utmost to set up the chore responsibilities when the kids are little. They are (usually!) much more obedient and respond better to positive praise, and if they know they have chores to do when they're three, they won't balk at doing them when they're seven. It's just part of their daily routine. Asking a seven-year-old to suddenly start doing a lot more chores doesn't mean they won't get done, but there will likely be a lot of grumbling that could have been avoided. It's even harder to implement when they're teenagers, so start when they are young!

Besides, toddlers love to help out, and just as they can take their toys off the shelves, they can just as easily put them back! They'll do cleanup as soon as you start singing the cleanup song, and it's a lot of fun to turn it into a game. Luckily for all of us, they don't see it as a chore, or work.

Our kids also know that they're responsible for their own rooms. I'll run the laundry once a week—I just put it in the baskets and the kids take it up and put it away. Even Dax and Paisley, from a young age, can hang up most of their clothes on their own. They're really good at matching up their socks, too!

ONE OF THE BEST WAYS TO GET THE CHORES DONE IS BY CLAIMING "ENERGY DRAIN"

We've tried various ideas over the years to get the kids doing their chores, because sometimes methods work for a while and then…they don't!

One tactic I like a lot is what I call the Energy Drain. This is another great tool I learned from *Parenting with Love and Logic*. This is what I use if I go into one of my kids' rooms and see a mess on the floor that needs to be picked up. I can pick the items up, but that child then needs to earn them back. So I put the items that were all over the place in a bag, and then my child has to *earn* then back by replacing my energy doing three extra household chores. All because I expended my own *energy* having to deal with their mess! That method works really well for my kids.

Except…when it doesn't!

Recently, all my strategies for getting the kids to keep their rooms clean had failed. Time for some tough love, so I wrote them this letter:

Dear Teenage Children,

I'm writing to let you know that despite my best efforts to teach you to clean up behind yourselves, I seem to have failed. I have asked nicely, politely, and kindly for you to clean up your rooms, but my pleas have been ignored.

I want you to know that I take no particular pleasure in reminding you multiple times a day to put trash in your garbage can or to put socks and underwear in your laundry basket. I don't love finding your beds unmade, your homework strewn about, your bathroom mirrors splattered in toothpaste, your countertops covered in makeup, or your clothing from last week sitting in heaps on the floor. I feel frustrated when I see my personal items splayed out in heaps around your room and bathroom instead of in my nicely organized spaces in my own room/bathroom.

I take no pride in my behavior when I begin to act frustrated and stop using my "nice mom voice" and instead begin to exhibit behavior unbecoming of someone who does truly love *you and wants to be an example of a nice human being.*

So the time has come for me to give back my *personal ownership of your room and belongings and instead allow* you *to own the messes.*

I'm going to do this by allowing you opportunities to demonstrate your cleaning abilities, and then let your own actions dictate your consequences.

From this moment on, the new house rules are as follows:

To make sure we all understand and agree on what "clean" and "deep clean" mean, you will be asked to do a one-time deep cleaning (repeated as needed). This consists of:

Wash your sheets.

Clean under your bed.

Vacuum the carpet and carpet edges, including under your beds.

Dust your room.

Wipe any grime, dirt, makeup, food, etc., from the walls, doors, and light switches.

Wipe all your baseboards.

Clean and organize your closet, rotating out clothing you either don't wear or have outgrown.

Put away all clean laundry.

Organize and clean your bathroom cupboards/closet/shower items.

Clean and wipe down all dirt or grime from the furniture in the room.

Clean and organize any and all drawers in the room.

When these items are done, you must demonstrate your ability to keep the room "clean," meaning picked up and generally organized for one week.

During this one-week deep-clean period, there will be no friends, Netflix, date nights, etc., until the week has been successfully completed. However, you have the opportunity to earn days off the seven-day waiting period by doing extra jobs to demonstrate your proficiency in cleaning. For each job you complete (subject to my approval and inspection), you will reduce the period by one day. You do not get to pick which days of the week you get off, as they will fall in order (M Tu W Th F Sat Sun). These extra jobs consist of:

Cleaning and organizing one half of the kitchen cupboards.

Organizing the kids' book closet as needed.

Organizing the attic.

Weeding the front yard.

Weeding one half of the backyard.

Running and folding all the laundry.

Organizing the food pantry.

Sorting and cleaning out the babies' play room.

Cleaning out and wiping the refrigerator.

Organizing and sweeping the patio and outside area.

Sweeping out the garage, including organizing bikes, toys, storage shelves, etc.

Completing other tasks as needed by Mom or Dad.

Thereafter, each time you ask me if you can go to a friend's house, watch Netflix, go out to dinner, on a date, or any other non-school/church-related activity and assuming the family schedule allows for your activity, I will enter your room/bathroom and assess its hygiene. I will be looking for consistent basic cleanliness and that your items are picked up.

If your areas are clean and organized, my response will be yes. *If the areas are not clean, the response will be* no. *There will be* no *second chances on the same day. Tomorrow is a new day.*

I will no longer argue with you, or nag you, to keep your rooms/bathrooms clean. Rather, I will allow you to decide how important those activities are to you as demonstrated by your actions within your room/bathroom.

I'm looking forward to a cleaner house and you are looking for a much calmer mother. ☺ It's a win-win for all of us.

XOXO,

Mom

Like any good mother, I taped this letter to the outside of each bedroom door and then waited. I knew the kids would not react well, so I spent a little time making sure I was prepared with calm comments and reactions in response to their outbursts. Sure enough, the kids came home, read the letters, and began to conspire, whine, overreact, etc. At one point, I heard a whispered "Passive-aggressive, much?" from one of them after they finished their letter. There were plenty of eye rolls. I kept my cool and just nodded and reminded them they wouldn't be enjoying the weekend until what I asked for in the letter was done. After about thirty minutes of complaining, my kids recognized that their actions were not going to change anything, and soon things were moving along as I had hoped. Each of the older girls finished deep-cleaning her room that day, and most of them had completely worked off their seven extra days within a day or two. I got to enjoy a consistently clean house for once and they did, in fact, enjoy a much calmer me!

MONEY AND ALLOWANCE

Shaun: "My parents tried to teach my sisters and me entrepreneurism at a young age. I even had to pay to watch TV, because my parents thought we were watching too much! They would give us a dollar in dimes, in a baby food jar, at the beginning of the week. A bigger jar was on top of the fridge. For every half hour of TV that we wanted to watch, we had to take a dime out of our own jar and put it into the big jar. What we didn't spend on TV during the week, we were able to keep for ourselves.

"Instead of just restricting the TV viewing, they were very wisely teaching us about opportunity costs. I could choose to watch an hour-long show; what was that opportunity cost? A full twenty cents! It didn't take long for us to figure out that if we spent all of our dimes on TV shows, and then we wanted to go to the store for a candy bar that cost twenty-five cents (money went a lot further back then!), our parents would say 'You're out of luck.' The less TV we watched, the more money we could save. My parents also told us that if we wanted to watch the news, it was free. I remember sitting down and spending a lot of evenings just being mad at Walter Cronkite because I had no money to watch the shows I really wanted—but I did learn an incredible amount about what was going on in the world while saving my money, and that was the whole point!

"So we don't make our kids pay to watch TV, but we've tried to come up with our own type of opportunity-cost system that keeps our family functioning well.

"If our kids get paid anything, it's income, and we usually give it out once a month for the older kids. The little kids get quarters if they do their jobs and their chores, but if they don't do their assigned tasks... it's not an automatic payment. The parental ATM has shut down!"

Our children have always completed chores in exchange for what we all know as room and board. By taking on additional jobs, longer-term assignments unique to them, they can earn income. We want our kids to understand that in real life, there's a cost to everything. Every service you render could bring in income, yet with that income comes expenses. We used to have a chart that listed what each child's income was and what their expenses were. Starting when they were five years old, if they were invited to a birthday party, they had to contribute a quarter or fifty cents of their own money toward the gift we bought. If they wanted dance or gymnastics lessons, they contributed nominally to that on a monthly basis. If they wanted an unnecessary ice cream, or a toy, they were expected to pay for that completely on their own. We wanted the kids to pay toward those activities so that they could feel a sense of accomplishment in what they were participating in, and also what it feels like to have expenses.

It is interesting to see their little minds finally grasp the idea of opportunity cost, and begin prioritizing their expenses to reduce costs and increase their savings. This is a life skill that will serve them well, especially when they want to download apps or join monthly services, such as Netflix, Hulu, Spotify, or Apple Music, that only cost a few dollars—and then see the monthly bill, where suddenly all those little downloads can become quite costly. When they understand that saved money can essentially make them interest, without having to do anything, they almost can't believe it. Then they want to save everything!

HARD WORK, PAYING OFF

Brooklyn, Bailey, and Kamri work really hard, in school, at their after-school activities, on their YouTube channel, and on their singing and performing. Many of their peers (and even adults) look at us and think, *Oh, I wish I could do that*, or, *Oh, you're so lucky*, and all that. Sure, there's a little bit of luck, but it's 99 percent hard work—and their fans and followers don't see that hard work. Just the end result of all the hard work. What viewers see in a video is the tip of the iceberg.

People forget that we run a business. Marketing, legal, management, finance, creative, production, post-production, and photography are a part of our daily work routine. A five-minute video can easily require thirty hours of work before the viewer ever sees it, and that is only the video side of our business. We often have about ten other projects going at any given time. This sometimes grueling schedule forces my kids to be more focused. They don't have extra downtime to spend idle or getting involved in a lot of the normal school drama. They have learned to work smart, prioritize their time, and really understand the value of money more than most teens their age. We've simultaneously had conversations about checking accounts and how to use their debit/credit cards while also discussing equity in companies, stock options, vesting periods, and more complicated financial matters.

Because we started teaching the kids about money at such a young age, I think this helped our girls tremendously a few years ago when their own careers started to take off. With the twins, let's say a brand deal comes through for $10,000, and at first they are thrilled and think, *Wow, ten grand goes a long way toward college!* But then Shaun sits down with them and discusses how out of that fee, a fixed percent goes to their manager, another to their agent, another to their accountant, another to their attorney. Then there are internal employee costs, prepayment of taxes, and the amount they can put away for college gets much more whittled down. (We always encourage giving back as well, via a tithe to our church, as well as other charitable organizations.) When you run the finances through that pay funnel in front of the girls, their eyes get big as they recognize that there is a definite cost to business. It isn't ever topline gravy, as we all wish. They then become more engaged in finding ways to effectively reduce those costs, and we know that those early lessons about expenses have taken hold.

My girls also are involved in conversations about using profits to reinvest in their other projects, such as their branded merchandise, music, or their newly formulated mascara product. They are learning that it takes hard work, as well as financial investment, to make more money.

Outside of savings, the income the girls take home is more than enough for movies and nights out, or to get ice cream with their friends. They buy laptops for school with it, and have their own Amazon Prime accounts. Their income also helped them pay for half of their car. The girls work hard and they deserve to have the income they work for—they don't want for anything, but they are very careful with what they have. Because of their early exposure to budgeting, they're now able to be involved in much more professional-level conversations about finances, and they understand how to manage their own money and their 401(k)s. This is a life skill that's invaluable, and will hopefully serve them and their own children well into the future.

Tips for teaching money management:

- Start them young.
- Don't pay for normal household jobs.
- Offer to pay for them to do EXTRA jobs around the house.
- Have them begin to pay for small expenses. We had our kids pay twenty-five cents toward birthday gifts for friends when they were very young, etc. This was a super-simple way to keep them involved and aware of their own finances.
- Don't be afraid to involve them in conversations about money
- Allow your kids to pay for some of their own privileges such as Spotify, Netflix, and their phone. Kids take care of and appreciate things more when they have skin in the game.
- Gradually increase the cost of items to your kids, along with their income, just as seen in real world inflation, and continue the financial conversations as they get older.
- Be real with them about money, and its benefits and pitfalls.
- Learn how to say the words "we can't afford it."

BUDGETING FOR YOUNGER KIDS

These are what we expected the kids to budget when they were between the ages of four to ten. All the math was doable if they were smart and careful with their money. We wanted it to be doable but challenging, so they actually had to think about their money and how they spent it. They also had money from birthdays and grandparents and from earning money for extra jobs. We paid them one month before we started to charge them their "bills" so they were always just slightly ahead. If they ever overspent they could also borrow money from us but we had them pay it back with interest. Where we list things like "bike repairs" or "lost or damaged items," we were trying to encourage them to be responsible and take good care of the items they were given—we would cover normal wear and tear.

4 years ($1.00/week)
10 percent tithing
10 percent savings
$.25 per friend birthday gift
$.25 per Christmas gift for siblings
$.10 per light left on or front door left open

5 years/preschool ($1.25/week)
10 percent tithing
10 percent savings
$.25 per friend birthday gift
$.25 per Christmas gift for siblings
$.25 per movie treat or road trip treat
Pay for lost or damaged items (within reason)

$.25 per month for violin/piano

$.10 per light left on or front door left open

6 years/kindergarten ($1.50/week)

10 percent tithing

10 percent savings

$.50 per friend birthday gift

$.50 per Christmas gift for siblings

$.50 per movie treat or road trip treats

$.50/month for violin/piano

Pay for lost or damaged items (within reason)

$1 for school clothes

$1 for school supplies

$1 for any field trip

$.10 per light left on or front door left open

7 years/1st grade ($1.75/week)

10 percent tithing

10 percent savings

$1 per friend birthday gift

Any bike repairs

Any lost or damaged item

School field trips (up to $2)

$5 toward school clothes/supplies

Extra school supplies (after initial school supply purchase)

Movie or vacation treats (dollar store)

Any extras for fun

$.25 for lights left on or doors open

8 years/2nd grade ($2/week)

10 percent tithing

10 percent savings

$2 per friend birthday gift

$1/month clothes

$1/month piano

$2 for regular school supplies (one-time fee)

Lost or damaged items

Bike repairs

Christmas gifts for siblings

School field trips (up to $2)

Movie or road trip candy

School signups (bags or candy, plates, etc.)

$.50 for lights left on or doors open

Late fees at library

$7 toward school clothes/supplies

9 years/3rd grade ($3/week)

10 percent tithing

10 percent savings

$3 per friend birthday gift

$2/month clothes

$2/month piano

Lost or damaged items

Bike repairs

Christmas gifts for siblings

School field trips (up to $5)

Movie or road trip candy

School signups (bags, cups, etc.)

$.50 for lights left on or doors open

Late fees at library

Gas to reimburse Mom for extra trips

$10 toward school supplies/clothes

10 years/4th grade ($4/week)

10 percent tithing

10 percent savings

$4 per friend birthday gift

$3/month toward clothes (if any)

$3/month piano

Lost or damaged items

Bike repairs

Christmas gifts for siblings

School field trips

Movie or road trip candy

School signups (bags, cups, etc.)

$.50 for lights left on or doors open

Late fees from library

Gas to reimburse for extra trips

$13 toward school supplies (for the year)

$2/month toward optional pizza day

$2/month toward contacts (if needed)

Contact solution

Chapter 10

The Family Squad

In this chapter, I'm going to show you how to apply your house rules to day-to-day living.

Our job, as parents, is to give our children the best opportunities to succeed, but parenting is not one-size-fits-all. Even if you have only one child, you'll still want to tailor your strategies to their unique personality and needs—and come up with new ones that might have you thinking outside the box.

We found this to be true early on by having twins. It would seem likely that identical twins would act the same, or that you could parent them exactly the same, but it became apparent early on that each twin had her own unique personality. One twin needed more sleep, for example, while the other twin required more food. One twin could ride a bike sooner, while the other twin learned to read earlier. We couldn't simply assume they would both do everything exactly the same, and we had to adjust accordingly.

All aspects of parenting fall into a similar concept of one size does *not* fit all!

"TEACH AND GOVERN"

Having six kids is a wonderful reminder that the world doesn't revolve around one person. Everyone is expected to pitch in, everyone helps, and everyone can have fun. Tonight might be Kamri's basketball game, and tomorrow, Rylan will have gymnastics. Everyone has a turn, and no one is ever fully the center of attention for days on end. We're all in it together, and that's what makes us root for each other to succeed. Our church often emphasizes the need to "Teach and Govern," which is a concept you often hear in the business world and that our church has emphasized for as long as I can remember. This means that parents need to *teach* children correct principles, and then let them *govern* themselves using those principles. All you can do is your very best to try to teach them the right way, but you can't force things. Children have their own agency. They won't always make the right choices, and they'll have to learn from those mistakes.

I hope that "Teach and Govern" will become one of your most important family rules. Children are smart and capable and will rise to the occasion when you trust them, and they *know* you trust them. Even Paisley, who's really young, knows that she's responsible for picking up her toys. Our children need the freedom to grow, explore, make mistakes, and deal with the consequences. They also need you to give them the necessary tools to go and create within the framework of their skills. If they've been taught well, they will govern themselves.

This is especially important in our digital age, where our kids see so much disrespect online—from their peers as well as from adults—yet those who are disrespectful aren't held accountable in most circumstances. That's been especially prevalent in the digital world recently, where some of the biggest YouTube stars are boys that disregard rules, cultural norms, laws, and even the sanctity of life in their videos. (One in particular, an extremely popular YouTuber named Logan Paul, caused a furor when he was in Japan, hiking at the base of Mount Fuji in what has been called "The Suicide Forest," stumbled upon a man who'd recently committed suicide, filmed it, and *joked* about it. Many of his fans are children, so this was even more shockingly offensive and disturbing, as he had to assume that young kids would see this.)

THE NOTION OF ENTITLEMENT

There's also often a sense of entitlement coming from our kids in this digital age, whether it's the mean girls or the spoiled kids who know that Mommy and Daddy will do whatever it takes to make any unpleasant situation go away. When I grew up, we didn't have a lot, and neither did Shaun's family. But we both had enough and we felt rich. Today I believe that social media has made entitlement worse as it paints a false image in the minds of children as to what is normal and not normal. The "perfect" photos posted on Instagram reinforce to children that they, too, should be entitled to the beach vacation and the perfect tan, whether or not it really makes sense for your family or your budget. Social media stories and videos of children acting out at school, doing drugs, or engaging in other risky behaviors and getting away with it present the idea that this type of attitude is normal and even desirable.

Sometimes even parents reinforce the behavior by allowing their kids never to feel the consequences of their actions or even condoning the bad behavior as "kids will be kids." A few years ago, some students who tested positive for drugs at our twins' school had zero consequences when their parents challenged the legality of what had happened. It was frustrating for the school, especially as the students who had followed the rules could see the lack of consequences for the kids that had broken the rules. Fortunately, the next year the school made all parents sign waivers clearly spelling out what would happen to any student found with drugs or positive drug tests. Should that have been necessary? No, but it was a very valuable lesson for our kids to see what happens when parents don't know how to let their children feel the consequences of their own actions.

BUTTON PUSHING, FAIRNESS, AND SIBLING RIVALRY

As cute and adorable as they can be, your children will have you second-guessing your parenting skills as they grow older. They'll most certainly learn how to manipulate you and their situations to get what they want. It's crazy to see how early they can do it, too! Then, as you add more children to the family, new challenges will arise as you learn to navigate kids dropping the ever-frustrating "it's not fair" phrase, or how to effectively referee die-hard competition or animosity between two or more siblings. Can they just go back to being adorable babies?

Your Kids Will Always Know Which Buttons to Push

Kids come out of the womb with distinctive personalities, but all kids are born with a very particular sixth sense: the magical ability to find your weak spots and push the button guaranteed to send you over the edge.

One of my biggest failures as a mom is being caught up in the day-to-day management of my family too often. There are six kids, and Shaun and I both work; we're both constantly micromanaging in an effort to keep everything functioning. There are a lot of pins to juggle.

Sometimes, I focus too much on the details and forget to let things go and throw caution to the wind for a day. I should relax more and enjoy the small moments more often. My kids have figured out that if they turn on one of my favorite shows, like *Downton Abbey* or *Victoria*, I will usually stop working, make the popcorn, and enjoy talking history and watching good girly shows curled up under a blanket with them.

One complicating factor for us is that, in addition to the normal give-and-take with siblings and parents in a large family, we also have to work alongside our kids and are juggling the roles of parent and manager. Sometimes, we have to say, "Okay, we're going to have a meeting right now. This is boss time, and then we'll go back to Mom time." You can't confuse the two. I always have to know when it's a button-pushing kind of day—like, for example, when the kids are stressed out from school or hormones are causing their skin to break out—and assess whether I need to back off and push the gas some other day when they'll be able to handle working.

What I also realized is that the kids often just need acknowledgment or validation. They're pushing buttons because they need us, and it's up to us *not* to click into our default response button especially when we're tired or stressed. I also find that usually when kids start button pushing, I can insist that they eat and get some sleep—and almost always the button pushing will stop. Kids need mental and physical downtime to regroup and re-center just like adults do. It is a healthy brain reset.

Life Is Not Fair

I can still so clearly see my mom's face as she looked me in the eye when I was a little girl and I'd go crying to her, upset because I thought my sisters were getting more favorable treatment than I was. "*It's not fair,*" I'd say to her with tears in my eyes.

I don't know why I bothered, because I always knew her reply would be the immortal "Who told you that life is fair?"

At the time, I just didn't get it. I remember thinking, *It's not fair that life's not fair! What are you talking about, Mommy? If you love me and you love my sisters, then you should treat us all the same! It's just not fair!*

It wasn't until I had my own kids that I realized you love them all deeply and equally, but not *really* equally, because they're all different. You love them equally, but in the ways that they need to be loved. The type of attention that Child A needs vs. Child B isn't going to be the same, not even for identical twins. One might need more quality time. Another one just wants to be told they're doing a good job. One might be struggling academically, so the one who's a straight-A student doesn't need as much homework time right then, and that can create a temporary imbalance of attention and time giving.

In our home, "fair" pertains only to their rights within our home. Rights include food, shelter, clothing, medical care, and love. Those items come unconditionally and as part of being a member of our household. Each child receives fair amounts of these things and can expect that we won't withhold those items.

A privilege, however, is different. A privilege is the ability to receive extras based on behavior and the individual family's budget. Things like a cell phone, or dance lessons, or computers, or friends over on the weekend. These items won't always be fair. Just because Brooklyn was ready for a cell phone at thirteen didn't mean that Rylan was. If Kamri gets friends over one weekend, it doesn't necessarily mean that all the kids do. These are tangibles that are given and taken depending on the children's ability to demonstrate mastery of certain skills, adherence to the rules within the family system, or the family's own ability to afford those items. In a Pinterest or Instagram world, everything looks perfect and seems like a right. Children have a hard time distinguishing between the two. Even parents can fall into this trap by putting extra pressure on themselves to have the dream house, the trendy furniture, the most expensive car, the over-the-top ridiculous birthday party for a two-year-old, in an effort to paint the ideal image of perfection for their own socials.

In our home we try to emphasize the idea that fair just doesn't exist. Daxton has required as much attention as almost all the girls put together, which has necessitated an immediate and ongoing response from us, and he needed it from a young age. Is it fair? No. Is it necessary? Yes. Will the kids understand? Yes. They might grumble, but deep down, as long as you are fully honest and explain, they *will* get it. You always have to be truthful to the other kids and say, "Look, I know this happened when you were this age, but here's the situation now, and we have to bend our rules to make the business of our family work smoothly. Just because the rules are changing doesn't mean I love you less and him more. It just means the situation is different."

Besides, anyone with identical twins has encountered the ultimate "It's not fair" scenarios.

Shaun: "I know how important this is, because I'm also a twin. Growing up, it was always Brande and Shaun, lumped together. I often felt like the second-class twin because Brande was the oldest. As a little kid, trying to figure out who I was could be difficult because of the feeling that I was just my sister's other half rather than my own, individual me. I spent a lot of time telling myself that it wasn't fair, and in fact, it wasn't. It was a lesson I needed to learn."

Knowing what Shaun went through led us to put our own twins into different classes as soon as they started going to school so that they could have their own sets of friends, people wouldn't call them by the other's name, and they wouldn't feel competitive with each other. But naturally, if Brooklyn got invited to a birthday party that Bailey wasn't invited to, or vice versa, we would hear endless complaints about the injustice of it all: "Why does she get to go and not me? I know Emily, too."

In situations like that, we had to say, "That's too bad. Life isn't fair. I'm sorry that Emily's mom didn't know there were two of you. Emily is Brooklyn's friend, not yours." Luckily, our girls have learned to navigate these situations pretty well. They still cross over with each other from time to time, but they definitely have their own identities and circles of friends and have flourished in them.

And then, what worked so easily for our first three kids just didn't work as well for the next two.

As soon as Rylan came along, followed by Dax, we had to rethink a lot of our strategies—they both broke the mold! Rylan's got such an amazingly unique personality and is her own little drummer. She honestly doesn't seem fazed by the fame of her three older siblings and that they're out there in public more. She also honestly doesn't mind that they have a higher profile; she has as much singing talent as Brooklyn and Bailey even though she really doesn't care about making videos or songwriting now, while they are in awe of her amazing confidence; she is going to be a real mover someday. The older three girls seemed to just fall in line with the rules where Rylan wanted to push the boundaries. Life was a giant game to her, and we quickly learned that to get Rylan motivated or interested in rules, we had to make things a game. With the older three, we would say "Clean up your toys," and they would. With Rylan, we had to say, "How many toys can you clean up in the next five minutes?"

Dax is thrice exceptional (with ADHD, all three subtypes, level 1 autism, and gifted intellectually), and the medications he needs to take to regulate himself suppress his appetite. So while the rest of the family is trying to eat healthy meals and do away with desserts, he *needs* to have an ice cream sandwich every night before bed, per his doctor's orders, just to get some more desperately needed calories in him. Sure, his sisters understand why, but I can see the "It's not fair" look glaze their eyes sometimes when they are craving a sweet treat at night.

Obviously, it's not fair...but that's just the way it is. At the end of the day, what's really not fair is why Dax has to be on meds in the first place. It is what it is, and we have to deal with it in our own way!

Understanding that life isn't fair *is* one of those lessons all children need to learn—in the analog and in the digital worlds. It's what helps them grow into themselves, to find out what they're good at instead of looking at others and feeling less-than. Why does so-and-so have such nice clothes, such a good singing voice, a bigger house, or a mom who doesn't work and never misses any of her sports events? Why does so-and-so get more views on YouTube for such unoriginal vlogs? Well, because life isn't fair. Never has been and never will be. It may seem harsh, but it's reality, and you can gently ease your children into that awareness before life knocks them into it. Let them learn this lesson when the stakes are low, and they'll be able to persevere in spite of it from a young age.

Sibling Rivalry

Tied in to the notion that "Life Is Not Fair" is the specter of sibling rivalry. As Shaun grew up as a twin, and as our firstborns are twins, we know a *lot* about it! We're very lucky that Brooklyn and Bailey have easy-going personalities and many of the same interests, so we had the typical sibling squabbles but have been spared any of the devastating kind of drama that can make raising twins or any siblings difficult. I worried a lot when they were younger that one would be better at grades or one would be better athletically and it would make the other feel bad. We've been lucky that by and large they have both been fairly equal.

When things have popped up like that, we have been extra-lucky that our girls have been supportive of each other instead of competitive. When the twins were in fourth grade, they both entered the school spelling bee. Naturally I practiced with both of them. During the spelling bee, the twins surprised us all by making it to the last round, beating out other fourth to sixth graders. Soon they were down to the top five and then the top three and then making the final two. As super-excited as I was, knowing that one of them would win...I was also nervous because I knew one of my daughters would lose. Back and forth it went for several rounds until finally Brooklyn misspelled something that Bailey got right, and Bailey took first place. I was so proud when as soon as Bailey spelled it right, Brooklyn ran up to Bailey, gave her a huge hug, and jumped up and down celebrating with her sister instead of looking sad for taking second place.

With siblings, you have to be a weather vane. That's what it is being a parent. Hopefully, the pole is fixed firmly in the ground (that's your "Teach and Govern" parenting pole), but every day, the weather vane up on top is going to be pointing in a different direction. You know you can't control the wind, so you have to be flexible. You learn that the essence of good parenting is that things shift, and not to assume that what works with Child A will work with Child B. You figure out what works for each child, so you can adapt and change how you parent and discipline each one in a way that will be most effective for them (and for you!).

Everyone comes with their own package of strengths and weaknesses—it's just that some kids are better at skills that are more visible. This can be a problem when one child has a unique talent or skill and another sibling doesn't, especially when it's something our current society has deemed valuable, like performing, athleticism, or modeling. I wish we would all talk more about and value other talents that are less apparent. Being kind, or patient, or organized is a talent. Rylan, for example, has an innate ability to keep cool even in stressful and intense situations, and that *is* a talent. It would be hard in a lot of ways to follow Brooklyn, Bailey, and Kamri, but honestly, it just doesn't bother Rylan. She's always just happy doing her own thing in her own way. What confidence she has, which is a talent in and of itself.

RYLAN, KAMRI, AND BROOKLYN, ON SIBLING RIVALRY

Rylan: Sibling rivalry doesn't just take place at home, although I'm not jealous of my older sisters. Brooklyn and Bailey were really good students; it's one thing for my teachers to expect me to be a good student or conscientious, but it's another thing to think that just because my sisters did something well in class means I can do it, too. That's not fair.

Kamri: There's some rivalry between me, the twins, and Rylan, because Rylan's a completely different person. She's actually a better singer than all of us, but we don't really compare our voices. I'm more of the instrument to her; I play the guitar for her and she'll sing for me. She just doesn't have the interest yet about running her own YouTube channel, but she's definitely become more comfortable with singing in front of people over the past couple of months. I've been trying to force her out of her shell. I'm making her record videos with me, and then I'll post them on Instagram or Snapchat, and then I'll show her all of the positive feedback. She told me she doesn't have her own channel yet because she doesn't even know what she'd do! But she is incredibly talented.

Siblings often do feel left out when there's twins, because twins are always going to have a certain bond; they're genetically and chemically connected. I was watching some home videos a couple of weeks ago and I noticed that the twins were always hanging out and playing together, and I was perfectly content sitting somewhere and playing with a toy by myself. I feel like I've always been like that. Just kind of fine hanging out on my own, and the twins have always been together, so it worked out.

Now that the twins are off to college, we all miss them, obviously, but it's nice for Rylan and me to spend more time together. As seniors, Brooklyn and Bailey were getting more attention. Especially over the past few years, we've had to do a lot of stuff for the twins when they went on tour. And it seems that they are always getting new clothes, and Rylan and I get their hand-me-downs. Only this year, because I grew taller than both twins, I am the one getting new clothes! Rylan is almost taller than they are, so the clothes may go from me, to Rylan, to Brooklyn and Bailey! I like that!

Brooklyn: Having social media, especially going on my phone, gives me an escape from sibling rivalries when we're all stuck in the house with each other.

QUALITY TIME NEEDS TO BE QUALITY TIME

With a large family and a successful business, we don't have a lot of time to spare, so we make up for our lack of quantity by focusing on quality. Quality time doesn't need to be long, but it does need to be hyperfocused. You must be present and fully engaged in the moment. You must listen without interruptions. Your kids will always know when you're not really there!

Once—okay, maybe more than once—I promised to spend some quality time with one of my daughters as I was finishing up some work. I was typing away on my laptop, and she started telling me a story. All of a sudden, I realized my daughter had been saying, "Mom, *Mom!*" for the past several seconds, and I asked her what she wanted. "You weren't listening, Mom." I apologized, and she went back to her story, but my mind soon trailed off because I just had to get out that one last e-mail—and I blew it again!

When you make the time for your children, make it for real.

Our kids know they all need to help out to keep the family going. If Shaun or I can't read to Paisley one night because of competing carpools, one of the girls steps in, and Paisley still gets the all-important book time and cuddles that help her wind down and feel loved before she goes to sleep.

Managing the multitasking has gotten easier over time. When Dax needed to practice reading and Paisley needed to be read to, I had Dax sit with me and read a book aloud to his little sister. He glowed with pride, and Paisley received quality time with both me and with her brother. The sibling factor allowed our family to accomplish more than we otherwise could have.

Still, spending enough quality time with children is one of the most difficult challenges working parents face, especially when the kids have a lot of after-school activities and are *busy* all the time. It's even harder when the kids get older and aren't at home as much. Luckily, we're often able to have our best Talk Time when we're in the car going to athletic practice instead of me reading to them at night like I used to do when they were little. Or your one-on-one moments turn into ten or twenty minutes in their bedroom, talking about whatever was important or bumming them out that day, and that often is exactly what the kids need to make them feel loved and cherished. You have to make the time, to take the time.

WHEN THE FIGHTING NEVER SEEMS TO STOP

What do you do when the infighting never stops? "She's breathing on me!" or "He's invading my personal space!" I have a couple of suggestions:

- Call a family council (see the next section) and talk openly about the behaviors you are seeing. If you are part of the problem, openly admit and apologize for it. Explain how the behavior and the chaos are upsetting to everyone, how the harmony in the home is lost, and ask the children for suggestions on what can be done to fix the situation. The key here is to listen, and let the kids offer solutions. You as a parent should only be guiding the discussion, not talking down at them the whole time.

- Praise your kids when they do get along. Positive reinforcement works much better than negative.

- Have the children go the next few hours completely isolated from each other. They are not allowed to speak with each other, eat together, or play together. You'll quickly find that by about halfway through the separation, they'll be ready to play nice.

- Implement a Job Jar. Nothing stops bickering more than assigning offending children the task of drawing from the Job Jar, full of up to twenty household chores on slips of paper. If they complain while completing that task, or continue needling the other children while they clean, tell them that they just earned *another* slip from the Job Jar. That works every time!

- I have often placed the bickering children into the farthest room from where I am working, telling them that they cannot come out until they say twenty nice things about the other, alternating one by one. Before long, you'll hear giggling and

laughing coming from the room, and when they prove to you
that they're done, they'll head off as better friends.

- Ever heard of a "get along" shirt? You can find these online. ☺
- If these all fail, and you don't know what else to do, call *Grandma*!

SETTING UP SUCCESSFUL FAMILY COUNCILS

A family council is a meeting where the members sit down for an
extended chat about a specific issue. This is meant to be an open and
honest discussion, not a blame session. Everyone should be involved—
even small children, so they know that their voice is valued. It's
important to set up parameters prior to the first council so that no
one child feels ganged up on. This is what we do:

- Plan the meeting in advance and clear everyone's schedule
  so that there are no issues interfering with it (such as a child
  needing to study for a big test the next day).
- Have a specific agenda. Councils usually work best if you
  tackle only one problem at a time. Usually parents lead, but
  children can, too, if they feel strongly about a subject.
- Meet in a quiet and comfortable location.
- Make sure the kids have snacks and water to drink, as a
  hungry child is a cranky child, and this can cause problems
  before you even start talking!
- Keep the meetings short and concise (especially if involving
  little children).
- Use a timer for the speaker, which helps keep things fair and
  prevents one child from dominating the discussion.
- Share responsibilities. One person can open, another can keep
  the timer, and another can take notes.

- Share a family cause. Is one child needing extra study time for a big test? Does one child have an especially important event? How can we help as a family?
- Use "I" statements instead of "you" statements, such as "I'm feeling like the house isn't staying clean." This prevents instant defensiveness from your children.
- Make decisions as a consensus. Try to allow children to come up with the rules and consequences so they feel ownership in them.
- If things get heated, anyone can call for a break.
- At the end, discuss positives as well as negatives. What was something that went well? Or that didn't?

TIME MANAGEMENT

More than anything else, my YouTube viewers ask me for advice on time management. Where does the time go, and how do we find the time to do everything we need to do?

To deal with our full schedules, we have family-planning meetings where we walk our older children through the week. Additionally, each night, Shaun and I go over the schedule for the next few days. We constantly communicate via text, and keep a shared family calendar online, which is a useful reference when I'm trying to figure out who's going where and doing what. This also helps when you have older kids that can see the schedule. More than once, Brooklyn has offered to run a carpool for me when she notices a conflict on the shared calendar.

This kind of diligent planning also allows us to schedule that all-important one-on-one time with each of the kids. If we take someone shopping or out for pizza, it can trigger the "It's not fair" whining from other siblings if you don't write them into the schedule, too!

Proper planning isn't just crucial for helping us manage our time; it sets a good example so the kids can see how to manage their own schedules. They understand that being late isn't just rude on principle; it actually impacts a number of other people in a number of different ways. It helps them understand that we're not just nagging them, but are, in fact, trying to make sure that everybody gets the same amount of time and consideration, and that being late means they're cutting into someone else's time. They can literally see how they fit into the family and think of themselves as part of something larger, and for the most part, they take that responsibility to the rest of the group seriously.

SCHEDULING TIME WITH YOUR OLDER KIDS

Even if they seemingly push you away, your older teens really do need you more than ever—not for physical caretaking anymore, but for emotional support during the years when they're figuring themselves out and have to deal with school and their peers and all those hormones and growth spurts. When I look at the twins' schedule realistically, they're gone so much and their days are so long that if we want to see them, it's often *us* going to *them*. So we take the time to go to the football games and watch the drill team on the field, staying until the end and taking photos. The twins still come home from a football game at 11:30 p.m. on Friday and I'm already in bed, but they know I was there, waving at them and screaming my head off!

In fact, when I go to the kids' choir performances or their dance performances—anything they're onstage for and I'm in an audience—at least once when I know that they're onstage, I yell their names or "Hi, smoochie-smooch!" *really loud*. It's become a running joke in our family. They all know it's coming, and their friends know it's coming, so it's like, "When is your mom going to yell at you?" At first, they told me how embarrassing this was, so one night I showed up and I didn't yell and they were almost upset at me afterward for *not* yelling! That's how I knew that my true motive for yelling was getting through—it was my way of letting them know that I was there supporting them; even if they couldn't see me, I could see them, and they could *hear* that I was there. And that's what mattered.

I have a friend whose kids have the same hectic schedule as ours, so she came up with a brilliant hack. She bought a bunch of foam-core posters with her child's face on them, and she sits in the stands during the games at school, waving the heads, which are easy for her kids to spot. She knows the kids can see them and relax in the knowledge that their mom is there, waving a head around! Your kids will pretend you're the most embarrassing mom ever, but in secret, they actually love it.

BAILEY AND BROOKLYN, ON TIME MANAGEMENT

Bailey: Because we have so much happening—college, work and family commitments, team sports, and Bible study—we have to designate time for each task, and then not venture outside of those lines. If you designate an hour to do schoolwork, you spend an hour doing schoolwork. You don't spend half of that time watching YouTube videos, and *then* start doing your schoolwork. If we don't do it in the time that we set aside...then it won't get done.

Brooklyn: My focus is always one step at a time. While I have long-term goals, I try not to plan too far ahead. Some kids can't do that, but if you can, try. If it's something that I can look forward to, then I try to plan for it, but if it's stressful, I try to never think about more than one day at a time because if I do, it can give me anxiety!

BAILEY, ON BALANCING COMMITMENTS

In our family, we know there are some things you can just *not* do. You have to help drive the carpools, and you have to sometimes help put the kids to bed or help make lunches, and it's just like another responsibility that you learn to work your time around. So when you want to hang out with friends, it's always "I have to finish my house responsibilities, how about we hang out at this time instead?" We've learned to schedule these chores and responsibilities into our calendar, so it's not like "Oh, suddenly my mom wants me to do this and I'm super aggravated by it." There are a lot of kids I know who don't have a job, or very many home responsibilities. If they do, they're *always* complaining about how their parents make them do all this stuff! Our calendar keeps us informed, tells us where we need to be, what we are to be doing, and gives us a good idea about how to prioritize our free time.

I know several kids at school who don't have strict parents, and can pretty much do what they want. They waste a lot of time, and get into trouble when they are bored. I feel like some kids are going to look back and go, "Oh, man, why did I waste my high school years acting like that or doing those things? What was I thinking when I made that decision?

Why didn't my parents tell me that was bad or give me a curfew?" I'm really glad we have these rules and boundaries in place in our family. At times they can be frustrating in the moment, but I completely understand their importance.

FITTING HOMEWORK INTO THE DAILY SCHEDULE

When Shaun and I were in school, all of our homework was done on paper. We'd carry our enormous textbooks to and from school, and get into trouble if we accidentally tore a page or left the book at home one day.

Today, once kids get to middle school, and sometimes sooner, textbooks and classwork have shifted from analog to digital, and homework often must be completed and submitted online. (The one exception is math, where calculations are still done by hand.) This wasn't an issue when the kids were younger and always did their homework at the kitchen table. If they had to turn something in on a computer, they also had to do it in a public area. We had that rule as we have a pretty tight control on what is or isn't consumed in the house through the Internet, as you know! Since the twins now need calm and quiet to concentrate, they're allowed to do their homework, as well as their work for YouTube, on their computers in their bedrooms. We trust them a little bit more—but we still have several other children who will sneak off and watch Netflix on their laptops or phones for hours on end! The struggle is real!

I have to say that going online can be an incredible aid to the kids when doing homework. If they're having trouble with calculus, for example, there are tutorials on many different websites that will walk them through the problem solving so they can figure it out. The Khan Academy has amazingly helpful tutorials and lessons to reinforce what the kids learn in school. The tools are just fantastic and make learning so much more interesting, especially with graphics and animation. When kids are learning about volcanoes, they can see actual eruptions online instead of just reading about them in a textbook.

This is especially useful for kids who are visual learners, rather than verbal ones—seeing images helps the information stick. We see this every day with Daxton, who is now a computer whiz and is teaching himself how to fly a plane on a flight simulator at the age of nine. He's also able to use a keyboard for his schoolwork as he has a hard time with cursive handwriting. So supervising the homework means paying a lot more attention, but the payoff is worth it.

If you find that homework is suffering because there are too many after-school activities, something has to give and it can't be the homework. Some kids thrive on challenges and can budget their time appropriately, and some can't. Don't force them to do activities because you like them (stage moms and soccer dads come to mind), but don't let them quit halfway through a semester or session unless their grades are affected or it's causing major distress—kids need to know they are responsible for their choices. You don't want to be a parent that your kids resent because you force them to do too much. You can't parent your kids to success in something you love or think is best for them. They have minds of their own!

TIPS FOR KEEPING THE KIDS FOCUSED WHEN THEY'RE DOING HOMEWORK ON A COMPUTER

- Keep the computer in the common area of the home so you can see what is happening.

- Create a routine.
- Regularly check the history on the computer to make sure your kids are staying on task.
- Review their homework assignments when they are finished to make sure all tasks are completed.
- Set a predetermined amount of time to do the homework before you spot-check it to make sure the child is staying on task.
- Allow the child to use earbuds to block out the household noise that might distract them. Some kids actually work better when they have a low level of music playing. If not, make sure the earbuds are not being abused—with music, for example, being too much of a distraction—and don't allow their use.
- Build in break times.
- Add incentives for homework done quickly, on task, and done correctly.
- Create a tech-free zone except for the items they absolutely have to have to complete the homework.
- Use parental controls and apps to monitor tech usage during homework time or to shut off other functions during homework time.
- Turn off notifications so that your child isn't getting distracted by all the other videos, comments, or texts popping up. Or turn on the "Do Not Disturb" option on their phone.

MEALTIME IS FAMILY TIME

We all know how important it is to eat together as a family, and we try really hard to make it happen, but it doesn't always work. You can't beat yourself up over it either, because you simply can't say no to the kids' school obligations, but they still have it instilled in their bodies that families eat together at a table—that food is about nourishment and meals are for talking about your day. Shaun and I both work full-time, so if I'm getting a complete meal on the table, that's as good as it gets. When I was growing up, my mom served our Sunday dinner in the dining room, with a linen tablecloth, two plates at each setting, and fancy utensils. That's not going to happen with us! Dinner-time during the week at our house may literally be buffet-style, where I cook the food and place it on the counter and the kids help themselves. It's quick and helps minimize the cleanup afterward.

If you have kids in different schools on different schedules, scheduling family mealtimes can be very difficult. For a while we tried to do breakfast instead of dinners—we figured that one meal together was better than no meal—and that worked until the twins went to high school and were getting up so early for preschool, athletics, or Bible study that they were out of the house before everyone else got up. Today, we really try to make sure that we spend time together around dinnertime, so we eat fairly early, right at 5:00 or 5:30, simply because the later it gets, the busier our evenings get. I found that if we eat earlier, we might get a chance of having most of us home, and it's better for the kids to do their homework on a full stomach. They come home from school very hungry, so either they're going to eat a big snack and we can't eat dinner until way late, or I feed them early and they have a good nutritious meal. Sometimes they are hungry again a few hours later, and get a nutritious snack before bed.

I have to admit that I don't hate cooking, but I don't love it either! I cook because it's cheaper and it's healthier as it allows me more control over what the kids are putting into their bodies. But don't get me wrong—there are plenty of nights where we're running behind and we order a pizza or something fast.

A major plus about cooking is that it exposes my kids to the how-to. Once I get going, it's great to have help and ask one child to stir-fry some squash and another to cook some rice. It gives us a chance to talk, and it also teaches the basic cooking fundamentals they should know before they leave the house for college or work. Many of the twins' friends have no idea how to boil water or make a baked potato!

TWEAKING THE SCHEDULE WHEN MOM AND DAD GO OUT: BABYSITTING GROUPS AND PJ PARTIES

When you and your partner need to go out at night, babysitters are a must—but they can upend your schedule as they are known to be notoriously lax at enforcing house rules. Kids quickly know their favorite babysitter is going to be the one who lets them get away with a lot of things you wouldn't let slip. They can also upend your budget with babysitters costing sometimes $8 to $15 an hour, or even more if they can drive, or you live in a big city, or when there are a lot of kids in the house.

The easiest way to deal with this is have a relaxed night away from House Rules. We often would adjust bedtimes to be a little later than normal, allow the kids to eat their choice for dinner (mostly mac and cheese or ramen noodles), let them pop popcorn or make muddy buddies to eat in the family room, and watch movies. This is a win-win for all—you are seen as the Good Cop, the kids can relax, and the sitter isn't stuck with a long list of rules that might be hard to enforce.

When you do have a babysitter, you need to make certain rules or priorities clear if they're important to you. It didn't bother me if the kids watched TV when the babysitter was there, but it really bothered me if I came home and my house was a mess and I had to clean it up. Some moms never want the TV on and want their kids doing puzzles and playing games, and they don't care if the house is a wreck when they come home.

DATE NIGHT BABYSITTING CO-OPS

When the kids were younger, we didn't have a consistent babysitter, and instead set up a babysitting co-op with three other couples with similar numbers of children and ages. It was a fantastic option for all of us in it, as each couple took one Friday each month where we watched everybody else's kids for four hours. We didn't have to pay for sitters, and the kids got to play together; it was like a party night for them, and they got to hang out and watch movies and eat popcorn with friends while Mom and Dad were on a date. They called it their PJ Party—and they still talk about it with fond memories.

Because I was usually the one setting up the groups, I was able to make the rules! Here's the paper I sent home with the other families:

PJ PARTY GUIDELINES

What: This is a babysitting co-op where each of four couples takes a turn watching everyone's children for one Friday a month, and then has three Friday evenings "off" to go out on a date.

When: Friday evenings from 6:30 until 10 p.m.

How:

- Please feed your children dinner before they arrive. Bring along any diapers, bottles, sippy cups, treats, blankets, etc., that will be needed.

- Generally we put all children under the age of four down between 7:30 and 8 p.m. and let the older kids stay up. So please bring a portable crib and any other item that is part of their routine.

- If you cannot watch the kids on your designated night, please call and make arrangements to switch with another family.

- If your kids are sick, please opt out of the PJ Party for that evening. If it is your turn to watch the kids and your little ones are sick, please switch with another family.

- Your turn will fall every five weeks (the fifth week of each rotation will be "off," when we will not do the co-op). This is the case even if you don't or can't drop your children off for whatever reason during the month.

- For the safety of the children, please ensure that both parents are home when you are watching the kids. If one spouse cannot be there, please have someone else there to help out (like a grandparent, a boyfriend or girlfriend, or a young person from your church congregation).

- If you have plans to go somewhere that do not fit into the 6:30 to 10 p.m. schedule, please just call and chat with the family in charge to make special arrangements.

- The co-op works best when tiny babies stay with their parents until they are nine months to a year old and/or no longer nursing.

- We will take breaks over Christmas and other holidays when people are out of town. Also, if any holiday (such as Valentine's Day, etc.) falls on a Friday night, we will skip co-op so that one family does not have to watch the kids on the holiday.

Having written rules and a structure to the co-op nights did make it easier for the kids to know what to expect, but it did take a while to work out the kinks. One of the little ones would have separation anxiety and cry for hours, or another would grab all the toys, but even when that happened, it was my turn only once a month, and my kids were taken care of the other three weekends. Fortunately, most of the kids got used to the system very quickly.

MAKING TIME FOR EACH OTHER

In addition to a date night once a week, Shaun and I try to go on a parent-only vacation at least every other year, even if it's only for just a weekend. We had been married for seven years before we took our first kid-less vacation, and we both remember feeling like, "Wow, we still like each other and have things in common outside of our kids!" Alone time is critical to reconnecting, talking about things besides the day-to-day, and having the intimate moments that are difficult when kids are around. Sometimes it is too easy to fall out of love when we let the schedule and kids overrun our lives. When you make an effort to go away together, it gives you a chance to look at the big picture and check in on how things are going from a much more relaxed standpoint. Taking a vacation with just the two of you can help you remember all the reasons why you fell in love in the first place.

FAMILY VACATIONS AND FAMILY TRADITIONS

Everybody needs a break.

A large part of parenting, if we're totally honest, is navigating what I call the day-to-day grind. You know what I mean, as I've said it already: Get up, make lunch, get the kids to school, make dinner, rinse, and repeat. So we firmly believe in instilling family traditions that give all of us not only a break and a change of scenery, but memories to cherish.

For us, one of the reasons we travel is to create what I call the Highlight Reel. When the kids are old enough to leave home, they're not going to look back and think, *Oh, my mom was such a good mom because she packed my lunch every day and did my laundry.* They're going to remember scenes from the family Highlight Reel that we have intentionally allowed to be recorded in their minds. The time we went to Iceland and swam in the Blue Lagoon with white mud on our faces, or the time we fell on the floor laughing because we walked into an "empty" hotel room only to find a man sleeping in our bed (the hotel had given us the wrong room key and number!). I still remember spending hours and hours running and climbing in the mountains around my family's favorite camping spots when I was little, or visiting orphanages in Nicaragua as a teenager and seeing a developing country for the first time. It was an incredible experience!

These family traditions, trips, and memories are going to stick in a way that what the kids do every day on social media never will. This is where you are striking the balance between analog and digital. Analog is your family structure and how you run your home and what you all do together. Digital is how you take advantage of websites to help you plan a trip and then share those memories with others. These trips and the memories that result are more important than anything else you can share on social platforms.

I don't think it matters where you go when you're taking the family somewhere. It can be camping in tents in the mountains, or in a rustic cabin in the woods, or a luxe hotel in Paris. For our family, we always go somewhere over spring break for a vacation that we know will create memories. We choose humanitarian service opportunities while we are there. I like going international because the phones won't work and data roaming is too expensive (or so we tell the kids), which keeps them off their phones and focused on family time. It's a lot to travel with our family of eight, but we're always looking for sites online with group rates that are so inexpensive, I literally couldn't take my kids to Disneyland for what I could fly them to South Africa for, all-inclusive! (True story!) Our best-kept secret is using Gate 1 Travel. Do some sleuthing and you can find incredible bargains, and there are many bloggers online who do the heavy lifting for you—just follow them and they put all kinds of deals online every day.

In the summertime, we have the most analog vacation ever when we go to a cabin in the mountains in Utah. On day one, the kids lie around and whine about how bored they are because there's no Wi-Fi and they can't use their phones and other electronics. By day two-and-a-half they're out building forts and playing games. By the end of the eighth day when it's time to go, they don't want to leave.

BROOKLYN AND BAILEY, ON FAMILY VACATIONS

Brooklyn: If there *is* Wi-Fi, all of us have a tendency to get distracted. It's really hard for us to take time with the family and put our phones down and away from work and friends. It's just as hard for our parents to put their phones down away from their work, too! Being a social media family, it's something we really struggle with, and it's why we try to take those vacations where we know we can't get online!

Bailey: The worst part for me on these trips is not being able to communicate with my friends. Just because I'd be, like, "Oh. I need to tell so-and-so about this." Or, "Oh my gosh, I can't believe this happened." I have to text so-and-so and can't. It never bothered me that I wasn't able to go on Instagram or Twitter. It only bothered me that I couldn't communicate with my friends about the cool things I was experiencing. But somehow the world kept turning, and they all managed to survive without me!

PART III

Friendship and Community

Chapter 11

Kids, Friends, and Bullies

One of the things I remember my mom telling me about parenting was that "the best thing you can do for parenting is encourage your kids to hang out with other kids whose parents are stricter than yours." She said it almost as a joke, but in all honesty, it's so true. When my kids have friends whose parents are stricter than me—suddenly I'm the best mom ever! Of course, the flip side of that is also true—if friends' parents are super-lenient, then suddenly I seem much worse to my own children and they get more upset when I enforce rules. I know that in reality we can't always hand-pick our kids' friends, but putting our children into situations where they are likely to interact with other kids who have rules and well-known boundaries is always going to be helpful for us.

Watching your children with their friends can be one of the greatest joys of raising them—seeing your little ones blossom into kind, compassionate, loving people who are there for their friends, and know in turn that their friends have their back. Like the time Brooklyn was inundated by friends coming over for two days after her heartbreak, bringing her favorite treats and thoughtful notes as they let her know she wasn't alone. It's especially gratifying when kids who have very different personalities learn how to get along with other kids who may be very different, too. Social media has had an incredible impact on friendship, bringing kids from all over the world together in marvelous ways that were impossible to fathom when I was growing up.

The flip side to that, of course, is when friendships go sour because of a miscommunication that has been evident due to digital dependency. Seeing your kids hurting can break your heart. And friendships can quickly become difficult to navigate where an offhand and innocently made comment on social media can quickly morph into an unintended drama.

So let's explore how we treat each other, in person and online, good and bad, besties and bullies.

FRIENDS AND CLASSMATES

Dealing with Digital Bullying

This is one of the biggest concerns that parents have today, so let's get straight into it. As long as there have been people on earth, there have been bullies. Look at what Cain did to Abel.

Most people are wonderful, kind, ethical, and naturally helpful. Some, for many different reasons, are not. Often, bullies are victims themselves and lash out in the only way they have been taught. They're not necessarily all bad kids. Some are just, in the heat of the moment, rude or unkind. That's not really bullying—it's just a normal human mistake. Full-blown bullying is something that's more chronic and deliberate.

When I was growing up, any bullying that happened in school, for instance, stayed in school. We could "shut it off" because it went no farther than what we did or where we went in our community. Now, as you know, bullying is a global phenomenon, and it's inescapable, online 24/7, and can be done by people hiding behind fake identities. Which means the digital age has added another layer to this issue: having to deal with the bullies you know and the bullies you don't know.

How We've Experienced Digital Bullying

Social media has shaped much of our own adult lives. As public figures who share many personal details, Shaun and I know that there is a price that comes with the benefits of popularity and an online career. We often have trouble dealing with that price: We always expected to be judged by strangers, but we didn't expect those judgments to be so constant and, sometimes, petty.

We first experienced the truly negative side of social media when we started a Facebook page for our YouTube channel, as I mentioned earlier in the book. Due to the high volume of comments on our videos, there were always a few people who said, "Your daughter has a big nose," "I don't like her hair color," or something similar. Fortunately, those had been pretty rare.

One day we started receiving a few noticeably weird comments that we later learned came from an adult man who was a predator pretending to be interested in hair content. At the time, we were barely making any money off the site, and after learning about the predator, we felt like the world was creeping in. We had been happily showing a mom bonding with her daughters and giving other moms ideas for doing hair in the morning, but all of a sudden, we were frightened. We blocked the man and had a long talk about whether or not to keep going, knowing that we had possibly seen only the tip of the iceberg that was (and remains) the dark side of the Internet. Obviously we continued on, after serious thought and a background check, but we were always more cautious and careful after that.

In another upsetting (but not quite as serious) incident, I once posted a video that showed one of my kids reaching out to hold my hand. I turned away for a split second because another child had said something distracting and my hand moved away from her. I got some sympathy from one mom: "Wow, it's hard to give all the kids attention when they're vying for it, isn't it?" I got one from another who wrote, "Wow, Mindy sure seems like a *mean* mom."

That comment made me cry! People didn't realize that what they saw in a short video on YouTube was only a tiny sliver of reality. Such snippets sometimes look better and sometimes appear worse than the reality of what they depict; some people take five hundred photos to get one carefully posed image of perfection, putting up an image like the gorgeous-pancake mom I mentioned earlier in Chapter 8, and some mothers momentarily neglect to hold their children's hands because they are taking care of another child.

A while after we had emotionally recovered from that incident, I posted an adorable video of me horsing around with the kids in the living room with the couch behind us. "What is UP with those PIL-LOWS?" asked one commenter. "They are SO UGLY. Don't you have any taste?"

That one made me laugh. I *like* my pillows, and a critique of an inanimate object isn't going to bother me. But even today, if someone goes after me or my children simply for the sake of being mean, I get upset! The golden rule should still apply online, but it often doesn't seem to. Being allowed to post anonymously doesn't give comment-ers the right to express a negative opinion about everything, especially not about children. Anonymity is a terrible gift to people who want to be cruel.

Some of you may be reading this and thinking we are crazy to keep doing this line of work, and exposing our kids to the dangers of the Internet. The truth is that *all* kids get this type of treatment and expo-sure, whether online or not. Our kids may get a larger dose, given that they have a larger presence online, but don't be fooled into thinking that these same exact things aren't happening in any child's world. I guarantee 100 percent that it is happening. In this age, with all the ultra-easy and pervasive digital access, it happens to everyone.

You Can't Control the Comments

The ease of leaving comments emboldens critics. You can't stop the trolls (people who comment negatively just because they can) from leaving ugly or deliberately hurtful comments. You simply have to avoid giving them what they want—a response.

I learned how to manage my feelings about being judged by strangers; sometimes the comments posted were so petty (yes, I *still* like my pillows!) that they made me laugh uproariously because they were so ludicrous, while others were genuinely hurtful. Growing a thicker skin became a necessity—especially nowadays when there are so many trolls and bots that many people have disabled their commenting feature altogether.

Our kids have grown thicker skins, too, by learning to place negative comments in perspective. If someone says, for example, "Oh, you're so fat," our kids don't internalize it as much as they once did. They've been exposed to it for such a long time that they can see the forest for the trees.

Tips to dealing with mean comments:

- Have *lots* of open conversations about what a mean comment looks like, how it makes you feel, and why it's important for kids to tell you about it.
- Remember that you don't know what's happening in that person's life, and they may also be struggling with an unseen issue.
- Teach kids they can't leave mean comments either. *Never feed the trolls!*

- Discuss your policy for answering hurtful comments (my suggestion is don't answer). Beyoncé once said, "Don't scroll down." You can also teach your kids that trick. Just don't scroll down through the comments.
- Wish the hater well. Often you will see an immediate switch from being negative to positive. A nice example of this is Chelsea Clinton's Twitter feed. She is the subject of hateful comments on a daily basis, yet when she does respond, it is always with kindness and grace.
- As I've said before, allow social media usage only on your digital device to begin with. This is a nice easy way to monitor beginner social media as you are constantly in and out of your children's accounts, and they know you are. We have dads who come to our meet-ups tell us all the time that they know all about us because their daughter uses their phone for socials, so they see what she sees.
- Disable comments altogether to avoid problems.
- Utilize the filters to help eliminate unwanted language.
- Take a cyber break if things are getting too hard. Go on a walk or enjoy some analog time.

Can it still hurt? Yes, sometimes. Does it stick? No. We continue to have very candid conversations about comments and the intentions of haters. We tell the girls time and time again that it's only a small group of people anonymously posting these hurtful and untrue things, usually in response to what they are struggling with inside. It's easier to hide behind a screen or even a fake identity and say whatever they want, without consequences. I think that if all platforms mandated that only verified, real people could post (and under their legal names), so much of the bullying would literally disappear overnight.

To be fair, I also think a lot of the cyberbullying that kids do is actually unintentional. It's just so easy to do it when you're typing text as quickly as our kids can type, and not really thinking. On another occasion, Rylan once left a hurtful comment online, and although it wasn't an extreme case, we took it very seriously and she lost her phone privileges for a week. (In kids' time, that's an eternity!) It was a natural consequence spelled out in her cell phone contract. She was upset at first, of course, but after a few days, she got used to it, and if she needed to contact me, she'd text me from one of her friends' phones.

BAILEY, ON ONLINE CRITICS

I think that, to delve into social media, you need enough confidence to ignore hurtful and small-minded criticisms. Let them roll off your back. It's a cliché, but it's true. If you know that you're not fat, or that your acne doesn't make you ugly, then you'll be fine.

Still, even with that confidence, it can be really hard because, as a teenager, you're vulnerable to the people trying to hurt you. At times, there's just enough truth in what they say to touch on your deeply held insecurities. Sometimes those people don't mean it, and sometimes they do, but gaining some perspective, seeing things from a higher level, really helps either way.

The advice I would give to my friends or others who may struggle is to always think of the commenter. What are they going through in their life that may cause them to hate on someone they don't know? If you think about the moments when you might judge someone, it is typically when you are feeling insecure about something they have that you don't. It is very often true that the spiteful comments are coming from kids and teens who, in fact, are the victims, whether they have low self-confidence or depression or more. In thinking this, it is easier to see those hateful comments as less of a jab at you and your appearance, and more of a cry for help or support.

Tips and Tricks

It's heartening to know that YouTube, Instagram, Facebook, etc., have added profanity filters to their platforms. (Go to the Settings sections of social media and follow the prompts, and see more information in the sidebar on page 224 in this chapter.) We take advantage of the ability to filter some of what our girls see. It can be an interestingly awkward experience for you—imagine sitting down and coming up with a comprehensive list of every swear word and offensive phrase that you've heard since grade school! This is your one-time pass to let your mind go as vulgar as you can.

BROOKLYN, ON WHEN DIGITAL BULLYING GETS OUT OF HAND

I'm on the dance team, and we have team bylaws that everyone on the squad is supposed to abide by, such as appropriate conduct, no using drugs, no drinking alcohol, etc. Some of my teammates were bragging about ways to get around the rules, and a few other girls let our coach know. She told the rule breakers, "This isn't okay. I know this is happening

and that it's all over your private social media accounts—
you can't deny it. I've seen it. You girls need to stop tweeting
when you're at a party. Stop doing these things or I'll have
to lay out punishments."

The girls making these bad decisions had each created
a second, private, Twitter account under an assumed name,
to hide from adults what they were posting and commenting
to each other—drug use, alcohol abuse, sexual activities, and
hard partying. One of our teammates saw a few posts, and
went to the director. All the girls in question were held accountable for their actions. You'd think that this was the end of the
story, but it wasn't. The girl who'd informed the director of the
private posts started getting shamed by the offending girls.
These girls said horrible things to her face and put threatening
notes in her locker, etc. She had done the right thing by telling
an adult, and she was horribly bullied as a result. This made
her question her decision to do the right thing, and she was too
scared to say anything about the harassment.

It came to the point that this poor girl was afraid to come
to school. It split our team in two. Many girls tried to support
the whistleblower, but we could only do so much, because
we couldn't stop the other group of girls from bullying her
outside of school.

For a long time, this situation divided the team, and the
girls who violated the rules continued cyberbullying the girls
who had supported the whistleblower and shifted the blame
to someone else. It almost seemed like the administrators
had their hands tied. They couldn't stop students from doing
drugs on the weekend; as long as those students didn't do it
during school hours, on school property, or post the activity
on social media, the school couldn't do anything about it.

It took several months for the team to rebuild, and I don't think the team was ever as cohesive as it had been, but it did slowly get better. Most of the bullies had learned their lesson, and many of the worst offending girls moved on.

During this experience I learned that social media can be used for both good and bad. While some girls used private accounts to create trouble, some of us used social media to identify and help our coaches see who and what was being a problem. We also used social media to send private notes of encouragement to our friend as she struggled through the bullying. It was super-frustrating to not have the school act quicker to make it stop, and even more frustrating that parents were denying it was their kids despite often having proof that it was. I recommend that parents keep a better eye on their kids and look specifically for their private Twitter or Instagram accounts because often those are the worst places for bullying to be taking place.

WHEN DIGITAL BULLYING CROSSES THE LINE

The biggest, and only, truly upsetting social media scare we've had in the ten years we've been online was Bailey's semi-stalker in the summer of 2016. This is her story:

Bailey: "I monitor our Twitter page because it's a smaller platform for us. Last year, I noticed one guy, whom I'll call Alex, commenting a lot on Twitter and YouTube, so I checked out his social media. He went to a high school near ours, was a few years older than us, and played football. He seemed normal.

"One day, I was driving home from Sonic with Brooklyn, and we stopped for gas. Brooklyn was at the pump when a car pulled up behind ours and a guy got out and started walking toward us. I automatically knew something wasn't right. Brooklyn felt it, too, and she got into a stance where she could kick him if she needed to. We both just instinctually felt that it wasn't a good situation.

"When he got closer to Brooklyn, he said, 'Hey, I'm a huge fan of your channel.' As soon as I heard that, I got out of the car so Brooklyn wouldn't have to talk with him on her own. He told us his name and that he commented on our social media a lot. I said, 'Oh, yeah, Alex, I see you on our pages all the time. That's cool.' I relaxed for a minute, but then he started asking us for personal information, like where we went to school and where we lived. I told him we couldn't say. Then he said, 'I noticed from your accounts that you go to Sonic a lot. Since I live near you, I've been going there every day, hoping to find you.'

"Of course we went to Sonic—it's hot in Texas in the summer, and we often went there to hang out with our friends and get a cold drink in the shade. He'd been waiting for us. He *followed* us. If we hadn't stopped at the gas station, he would have followed us home.

"He asked for our phone numbers. Again, we said no, explaining that our dad wouldn't let us give them out for safety reasons, but he persisted. Brooklyn got back into the car so we could get out of there, and I just wanted to get away from him so badly that I panicked and gave him my number. Big mistake. It was so stupid!

"We drove the long way home, making lots of extra turns, and I was terrified that he was going to follow us all the way. As soon as I got home, I immediately told my parents. I was so scared that I started bawling. My parents reassured me. I'd had a fight-or-flight reaction, and getting out of there fast was the right thing to do. It's a lot easier to change your number than to remain in a sticky situation. I felt a little better, but not really.

"Predictably, Alex texted a few hours later. My mom took over. She texted him that he had the wrong number and was texting some guy named Paul. He was disappointed, but the conversation ended. He sent us a letter with hearts all over it to our PO box, but that didn't worry me. A lot of our fans send us mail. We also decided not to post to Snapchat or Instagram in real time anymore and instead delayed our posts until after we had left that location. We had never enabled geolocating on our phones, but people could still figure out where we were based on what they saw.

"A few weeks later, we went to Cow Day—free food!—at Chick-fil-A. I had put a huge group together, and we were all decked out in cow costumes. We looked so ridiculous that my mom took a picture of us as we walked into the restaurant and put it up on Instagram without thinking. I was sitting at a table, having fun with my friends, when, about ten minutes later, Alex walked in. He didn't look at me or order food. He just sat down at a table that had a clear view of me. He didn't come talk to me, but it was like he was taunting me—'Let's see what you're going to do about this.'

"I went up to my mom. She hadn't seen Alex yet. I was freaking out. I told her to get me out of there. I didn't want to be in the same building as him. She said we all had to leave. Our giant group of twenty kids got up and went out through the exit farthest away from Alex. He went out the other door, ran around the building, and intercepted our group as we were hurrying to our cars. He walked up right next to me and said, 'Hey, I think you gave me the wrong number.' I could see my mom taking photos of him, and I said, 'I'm sorry but I can't give you my real number. I talked to my dad about it and it was a definite no.'

" 'Well,' he said, 'have you gotten my letter yet?'

" 'You mean the letter you sent to our PO box?' I replied.

" 'No. I sent a letter to your house.'

"That startled my mom, and we stopped short. 'How did you find our home address?' my mom asked. My heart was racing.

" 'Well, there's a website. You can pay a fee to get anyone's address,' he said.

"The letter he'd sent to our house arrived the next day. He talked about how he'd been teased for being fat when he was younger, how he tried to live life to the fullest because he never knew when it'd be over. He talked about death a little bit. He also put his return address on the letter. I realized a super-dangerous stalker would never do that. He was probably nothing more than a mixed-up kid making a not-so-great decision, but what he was doing still wasn't okay.

"My parents drove over to his house and took pictures of his car and license plate, and we notified our neighbors to be on the lookout for his vehicle. We installed cameras on the outside of our house. We thought that would be the end of it, but a few weeks later, Alex showed up at our house when Rylan was babysitting our little brother. She didn't answer the door when he rang as we've all been trained not to answer the door when parents aren't home. She got really scared when he went around to the side of the house and peeked in the windows to see if anyone was home. As soon as Rylan saw him drive off in the car that our parents had seen before, she took Dax out the back door, climbed over the back fence, and ran to our neighbor's.

"Alex came by *again* later that day, but fortunately, my mom was home by then. When she saw him coming to the front door, she grabbed her phone and started recording. She'd already been told by a family member in law enforcement that she needed to have it on record that she was telling Alex to leave me alone, that what he was doing wasn't okay, and that he was never welcome on our property. After he left, my mom called the police and told them everything.

"We never saw Alex again, but within a week, something else happened. We had posted our regular Sunday night video on our family channel, and when my mom went to check how things were going, she noticed that a newly created account had posted our home address in the comment section. YouTube had taken the comment down as a privacy violation, but the account kept reposting it, and other people kept liking it and commenting on it. Sure enough, later that week, little girls with their friends and parents were coming to our house to drop off cookies and letters. As sweet as it was, it was happening at all hours of the day. When we were outside filming, carloads of people were driving by and taking pictures of us. Some of the girls rang the doorbell late at night when our little siblings were asleep and asked if my sister and I were home.

"My parents decided that the best course of action was probably to move. It was a terrible inconvenience for all of us, but it was necessary. We're much more cautious and prepared now. We have taken precautions to keep our address safer, and security around our home is tighter. We learned a lot in those interactions with Alex. We know it could have been much worse, and consider ourselves lucky that we've had only one mildly creepy Alex in the nine years our family has been online.

"Thankfully, we've encountered much more love, kindness, positivity, and fun than we've had negative experiences. We want to make sure we don't focus too much on the negatives—1 percent of our overall experiences—without appreciating the huge number of positives, too.

"You can't stop doing something you love just because you're afraid that something bad might happen. The odds of a plane crashing into you on your morning walk are much higher than the likelihood of you experiencing physical danger because of social media, but you still go outside!"

Tips and Tricks

You don't have be famous to have a stalker or someone who is paying too much attention to you in a way that makes you uncomfortable. Whether you're well known or not, it can happen at school, your workplace, or anywhere.

- Recognize that if you allow your account to be public, anyone can find and follow you. Be prudent about posting your location.
- Turn off your geolocation on all devices.
- If your account is private, make sure you know and *trust* everyone that you allow within your friends/followers.
- Don't post photos of the front of your home, especially if your address is visible, or of nearby street signs or other local landmarks.
- Be careful not to inadvertently expose your address by posting a picture that shows your mail. This commonly happens when taking selfies, when there is mail lying in the background.
- Never let anyone know when the adults in your household are going to be away for any period of time.
- Don't post in real time. Delay your posts so people can't locate you easily.
- Don't post about vacations while you are away from your home.
- Add your address and variations of your address into your social media platform's filters so that nobody can comment your address for others to see. (For example, if you live on 2267 Bakersfield Dr., add "2267, Bakersfield Dr., Bakersfield Drive, 2267 Bakersfield Dr." to your comment filter.)
- Use a PO box, or other mailbox service, instead of your own personal home address if you need to list an address publicly.

THINK BEFORE YOU POST (BECAUSE YOU ALREADY KNOW THAT THE INTERNET IS FOREVER)

In retrospect, we're very glad that we learned how careful we have to be of *what* we say and *how* we say it online, especially as a transracial family.

We don't talk politics, and we stay away from race, except to say positive, uplifting statements. We don't let our kids contribute to or discuss controversial topics on their platforms either. This isn't because we don't have opinions. It's simply because we've opted to create a space online where anyone can come and feel welcomed with kindness, respect, and love. We will receive people of any color, gender, religion, or political party, and love them simply because they are a human being who deserves it. We try to keep things that could be divisive out of the conversation.

Generally, it's easy to be a good citizen of an online community as long as you write only what you would be willing to say to a person, face to face. Online anonymity is a boon only to the kind of person who gives a mother a harsh look if her child starts crying in the grocery store.

HOW TO USE FILTERS FOR PRIVACY

Every platform has filters, found when you click on Settings, that parents can use to limit those words showing up in their comments. You can do this for comments on YouTube, Facebook, Instagram, and Instagram Live. When you find the filters, enter in all the profanities you can think of. We add our address and phone numbers as well. You can add your children's names if you want, too. Make sure to add various misspellings of words as trolls might say, "Send me a picture of your bobs" or "bobbs" (instead of boobs) just so it will get through the filters. This is an advanced trick, so be sure to look out for it. On YouTube, the filters will remove the bad comments from the public view, but still keep them for the troll so the troll won't even know they have been removed unless they log in under a new account. Filters are some of our best friends!

Bottom line: We need to stop being so hard on others and ourselves while judging what we see on social media. I had to admit that there are people online who have zero shame about posting whatever pops into their heads, and I had to learn to deal with it. So did our kids.

As time went on, we didn't see a lot of bullying so much as the gossip type of things where people will go on forums and get a little snarky. For instance, our girls are sometimes accused of using autotune for their original songs, and it's hard to convince people otherwise—as identical twins, their voices naturally sync so nicely together that it can sound like they're autotuned when they're not.

We also know that our viewers or followers are seeing only a very small percentage of our lives, and there's really no difference between our family and theirs, other than the fact that we turn a camera on. Our kids struggle with cleaning their rooms. We struggle with kids on their phones and with curfews. We don't have producers and writers. What you're seeing is what we're doing—just normal family stuff that isn't scripted. If Brooklyn and Bailey are fighting, the last thing we'd think of doing is turning on the camera! We show what we are comfortable sharing and nothing more. Recently we continued vlogging, and it wasn't until months later that we revealed that we had been dealing with Daxton having a difficult school year, going to many doctors, and discovering that he has autism. We could have vlogged that entire journey but opted to keep things quiet until we had time to process it as a family first. There's nothing different about us, but people perceive what they see in our short videos as being the reality 24/7. As the saying goes, perception is reality, and that's true online. Viewers often believe what they want to believe.

DIGITAL FRIENDSHIPS ARE AS REAL AS IRL FRIENDSHIPS

I've found that the positives of digital friendships are far more impactful than the negatives. As we learned when we went to Dubai, there are people all over the world who consider me and my children as friends, which is *incredible*! They are interested in us and they care about us, especially my girls.

Another plus about digital friendships is that they allow kids to stay in touch no matter where they are. When I was a child, if a friend moved away, it was very hard to keep the friendship going, no matter how close you'd been. Pen pal letters took a while to arrive, and long-distance phone calls were too expensive. Today, on the other hand, as long as you're online, your friends are as close as a click away. And our kids have become friends with many "virtual" friends who are as important to them as their real-life friends at school and church.

Let me give you an amazing example: Last year, we noticed someone put up a video entitled "Is Rylan the least favorite child?" The girl that made the video pulled negative comments from other people, compiled them into a video, and then at the end attempted to explain with video proof why she didn't think that was the case. She was on Rylan's side, but the first half of the video wasn't very positive. For whatever reason, this video took off virally—not intentionally, as the girl who made it did so only because she felt bad for Rylan, who is a total stranger, and was trying to make her feel better!

After we noticed what was happening, I pulled Rylan aside to ask her how she felt about this video, since many kids at school were already talking about it. She smiled and said, "Oh my gosh, Mom, I have had so many kids at school ask about this video! It doesn't bother me." Because real kids in real life are online all the time, they wanted to make sure the digital comments hadn't hurt Rylan's feelings and that her family really did love her.

I've already talked about Rylan's remarkable ability not to get ruffled. She went on to say, "I think this is *so* funny. It's *hilarious*! I just keep telling people, yeah, I'm clearly the favorite child!" And then she came up with a brilliant idea: "I think we should do a new video where I react to *that* video." So we did. It was hilarious, and her comments the entire time we filmed it were, "This is *so* ridiculous!"

Rylan's reaction to this situation was an excellent lesson for her siblings and friends. She could have become very upset by a virtual reaction to something she knew wasn't true, but instead, she recognized how the lovely girl who made the original video considered her a friend, and wanted to defend her to drama-creating haters.

DEALING WITH FOLLOWERS

In the digital world, for kids, having lots of followers on social media is a big deal—it's a status symbol and shows their friends and followers how popular they are. It's such a big deal that some kids even resort to paying for "fake" followers that are really bots just to impress their friends, especially on Instagram and Twitter. (Kids aren't the only ones who do so—when Instagram did a huge purge of fake followers in 2014, it was amazing to see how many superstar celebrities had paid to have fake followers inflate their popularity. YouTube and Facebook have gone through similar purges over the years, and Twitter has finally started purging computerized bots.)

We know firsthand how important followers are on Twitter and Instagram. Our girls have had people in the past that wanted to use them to get "InstaFamous" and gain new followers to up their own popularity. They've had friends say, "Take a picture of me, and make sure you tag me when you post it!" They wanted the photo tagged so that our girls' fans would see the tag as a sign that *this* person was cool or that they had access to unseen photos of my girls and follow them as a result. We are not okay with this, and the kids are not allowed to follow their personal friends on their work accounts. Shaun told the girls to use him as an out, by saying, "My dad doesn't allow me to mix personal and private accounts." (He likes to act tough!)

It's important that your kids know that they don't have to accept every request of someone to follow them. Our girls also have private accounts with only trusted friends and family on them, and they know that whatever they post there will stay in their small circle.

Be a Silent Follower

One of the biggest complaints kids have is that their parents "follow" them on apps like Snapchat and Instagram. To that I say, tough. You need to make it clear that if they want to use these apps, you need to follow them there, so you know what's going on. A huge red flag for any app is that kids don't want you there!

But if you are following your kids' social media accounts, you should be a *silent* follower. No teenager wants their mom telling stories about the time they pooped their pants at the zoo when they were little. You are there solely as a monitor to ensure your child is safe—*not* to have a voice or embarrass them. The only exception is if you occasionally jump in to support them. If my girls post something about making the soccer team, or passing a final exam, I might comment, "You're amazing, Kamri...happy to see your hard work paying off!" so she knows I'm there for her as her biggest cheerleader.

I don't recommend that parents follow their kids' friends' accounts or allow their kids' friends to follow them unless they are very, very close family friends. Your kids will see this as a violation of their privacy and feel that you're being overly intrusive. Your job is to take care of your kids, not to meddle with their friends' social media accounts.

WHEN KIDS ARE STRUGGLING, AND THE PARENTS MAY BE, TOO

Not that long ago, one of our girls' friends was involved in some bad situations involving heavy alcohol. We called the parents, and they seemed to be pretty receptive and grateful for the information…but then the behavior kept happening.

This puts you in a bit of a bind, especially if your child is good friends with someone who is dealing with the kind of behavior you can't approve of. You don't want to ignore it, but you're not the parent—and as we all know, one of the rules of parenting is that you can't discipline other parents' kids, much as you might want to! Instead you can only parent what is in your control, which is your own kids. In this situation we had to have several conversations about not spending as much time with this friend and whether our girls were comfortable around her now that she was making significantly different life choices.

Often, the conversations are started by our kids with passing comments about their friends. They may mention something they saw at school or someone their friend is now hanging out with. Or feeling sad about not spending as much time with that person. Sometimes I just overhear them discussing things on the phone or with friends. (Never underestimate the information you can glean by driving a carpool with multiple teenagers in the car!) I try to pick up on these conversations and use them as entry points to opening a full-blown conversation. Sometimes the conversations are difficult, like trying to explain why your child just may not be cool enough anymore in their friends' eyes. It hurts to see them hurt. And sometimes you are on the other end and pick up on comments where your child may be the instigator of a problem. Those conversations are also hard. We've had both in our family over the years.

In the end, our daughter's friendship with the friend who was drinking too much drifted to a natural conclusion. They remain casual friends, saying hi in the halls, etc., without spending the large amounts of time together as they did before. Though it may be hard and sad to make decisions like that, you always need to know when to move on if needed. Often these situations end up being just fine, with the kids and parents being good people who choose to parent differently, and that is okay. Families come in all shapes and sizes, and parenting takes on many many forms.

Sometimes, you just might not know the backstory; perhaps the parents were trying to end the bad behavior but not succeeding, and were growing weary by hearing about more cases like this from concerned parents like us. We all can think of cases of really good people who have really strong, sturdy, stable, loving families—with parents who've done all the things that they felt were right for each child—and yet they still have a child who turns to drugs or drinking or self-harm. In addition to being so worried about their kids, parents feel like failures. They fear they're being judged by other parents and friends. It's heartbreaking for everyone when this happens. Especially as one of the most common things these parents say is, "I never thought this would happen in our family."

As I've said already, one of the best lessons I've learned over the years is that you can't parent kids to success. At least half of what a child ends up doing in life is because of who they are. Your job as a parent is to help them find out who they are and where their strengths and weaknesses are, and to do your best to hand them the tools necessary to be a success.

The next step in being a good parent is stepping back and allowing them to fail.

Allowing them to understand the cost of behavior, as well. I don't mean that in a harsh way at all! Life lessons are about understanding what the cost is of all behavior. Usually, the cost is many dollars in the emotional bank, when your kids are working hard, being good friends, and navigating their way through childhood into a successful adulthood. You're there to help them learn the lessons and apply them, now and in the future.

At the end of the day, the best you can do is "Teach and Govern," and assume your children will make smart choices most of the time, and learn from any mistakes or mishaps when they don't! Boundaries and rules make children feel safe. Being preemptive and enforcing consequences help your kids make more of those smart choices. They can choose their actions, but they can't choose the consequences—that's up to parents as the Loving Enforcers.

KNOWING WHEN TO BACK OFF

How do you know when to step in and give advice? Sometimes, kids just want a sympathetic ear when they need to vent, and then you letting them say what they want to allows them to figure things out on their own. Kids are really smart when given a chance!

Other times, though, you might need to step in if the situation has the possibility of escalating. One recent evening, I could tell that Brooklyn and Bailey were both very tired and pretty stressed. They started sniping at each other and bickering back and forth. I tried to let them work it out and it seemed to be moving in the right direction when suddenly they were both quite upset with each other. I could see that this had the possibility of getting bad very quickly since both were becoming quite emotional. So Shaun and I stepped in and separated them by asking one to run an errand for us and the other to do something around the house. This gave them the space and air to let calmer heads prevail before the situation intensified to the point where hurtful things could have been said.

This is always a slim tightrope to walk, and is there a magic-bullet answer? Nope! Every parent is going to respond differently, just as every child may respond differently.

I feel it when my kids are hurting, but I don't step in very often unless it's fairly serious. Once our girls became teenagers, if they had a problem in class, I pretty much told them they needed to work it out with their teachers, to set up meetings or tutoring. Their high school very wisely makes it clear to all parents that they don't want to hear from us—they want to hear from the kids. If the kids are missing an assignment, they're old enough to start working out their own problems. I love this about their school.

I think that one of the hardest things as a parent is *not* to step in, pulling off the mother bear mask, especially when you can clearly see how to solve a certain problem, but to allow your kids to figure it out on their own. It can be hard to do this, because when there is teenage drama, our kids can veer from *I hate her* to *She's my bestie 4ever* in the span of a single afternoon! How are you supposed to know what advice to give? What if you inadvertently say the wrong thing?

I have to say that one of the upsides of being a full-time working mom is that I'm so busy that I can't dive into all the inevitable day-to-day dramas that come with growing up. When I was a stay-at-home mom, I had more time to stress about the little ones; now I don't get as embroiled in the day-to-day things, because I know that if it's a big thing, it will circle back. In the long run, my kids' knowing that I trust them to solve most of their daily problems not only gives them pride in their decision making, but also helps me to be able to step in with authority should I ever be needed.

BE SPONTANEOUS!

When my kids are having issues with their friends or just having a bad day or week, one of my favorite things to do is surprise them. It takes so little effort, yet it reaps enormous rewards—for you and the kids! It's a great technique that I learned from my wonderful dad, as mentioned earlier. Shaun has taken notice, and will pick up our kids' favorite fast food, including a milkshake, and surprise them at school with it. I often drop off bags of treats to the schools for the kids to hand out to friends, and I notice that our older kids are now doing things like this for their younger siblings.

Being spontaneous doesn't require that you spend a lot of time or money. Just do something unexpected. You send a text before or after school with a loving message of encouragement. You can show up after school or an activity one day and take your child out for a meal or to a store to buy something they've been craving. You can order something online and have the box waiting for them on their bed when they get home. You can give them a few "Get Out of Chores" cards you've written out that they can hand you when they don't feel like setting the table. Sometimes it's as simple as just making a little extra time to sit in their room and chat, which always lets them know you care about them.

Sending flowers like my dad did always works—when the girls tried out for the drill team, I sent flowers to the school and wrote "Good luck tonight" on the card. I knew this would have the most impact if the flowers arrived at school, rather than giving them to the girls the day before, and they were thrilled.

Now the kids have learned how lovely it is to be spontaneous with their friends, too, to congratulate them on special days, or when they need a pick-me-up!

A FINAL NOTE ON DIGITAL BULLIES AND TROLLS

Let's just be real for a minute, okay? Trolls, comments, and haters are some of the worst parts of being online. It's funny how a hundred people can leave positive, lovely comments...but the one I will remember is the ugly comment. There are entire forums online dedicated to nothing but ripping online personalities and bloggers apart. I used to pop in once in a while just to see what they were saying, but every time I would walk away feeling angry or frustrated. I literally just had to make the rule that I wouldn't read them. What's a bit stunning about the online forums, though, is that these people are obviously watching your every move, every video, every announcement because they can literally talk about *everything* from your online information—but sadly for whatever reason they've decided it makes them feel better to just vent with each other and obsess over hating people.

As I've mentioned already, I've definitely developed a thicker skin to some of the comments and we utilize our filters to keep a lot of the worst hate out, but still sometimes I see the craziest comments. The worst ones always start with a "Not to be mean..." or a "Just gotta be honest..." type of statement. I always tell my kids that if you have to lead into a statement with a disclaimer, it's *highly* likely you should just keep your mouth shut!

There is no perfect solution for this problem, and I don't think there ever will be. All we can do is try to lessen the blows for our children until they are more adept and old enough to handle them. When the comments come (and they will), teach them your best tips and tricks, love them a little longer, hug them a little tighter, and help them see that online comments do not define who they are. What's inside does.

Chapter 12

You've Got to Have Friends

It takes a village to raise a child, and it takes the same village to support the parents of that child! We all love to think we can do everything on our own, but the truth is that we can't. We are hardwired for companionship and friendship.

It's so important for you to carve out space for yourself in order to survive as a parent—and your friends can help you do it. Even when you have a wonderful and loving partner like I have with Shaun, sometimes there's nothing quite like sitting down and having a heart-to-heart with your girlfriends in real life (or IRL, as my kids would say!). Analog friends are the ones who you can call in a pinch or in a pickle. They're there for you when the car won't start and you have to pick the kids up from school. They're the ones posting flyers all over town when your dog runs off. They're the ones bringing you chicken soup when you've caught a cold that just won't go away. They're the ones listening sympathetically when you're upset about something that happened with your kids, without passing any judgment. They have your back. They're your posse, your squad, your tribe, your own mini-community.

FINDING THE TIME FOR YOUR FRIENDS

How do I find the time I need to spend with my friends?

It doesn't happen as much as I would like! You have to find time, to take the time, and it can be very difficult. That's when I say to myself: Making friends is easy. Being a good friend and *keeping* your friends is hard!

When my kids were younger, I was a much better friend because we would all take our kids on play dates, or to the park or library together. It was so much easier to hang out and have time to talk and catch up when the kids were having fun with their own friends. But when the kids get older, you're simply busier running them in eighteen different directions at once. Their schedules are so hectic, and then you get crazy busy, too, especially if you're a working parent.

I think what helps is developing touch points with different people and building friendships through your kids' activities. If I go to the soccer game, for example, I know I'll see mom friends there, and we don't have to call each other to make plans—we just show up! I also have one dear friend whom I work out with. She keeps me accountable for going to the gym every morning, and we have fun laughing, grumbling, and whining throughout our workouts together. Also, I find that my friends my age now like to plan Girls' Weekends Out, quick weekend trips together, where they get a break, play games, eat junk food, and have much-needed girl talk. They do not do this often, but at least once a year. This gives everyone a chance to recharge and have fun without worrying about the hectic schedule of home life for once. Some of my favorite recent friend memories are with my girlfriends huddled up in a cabin and playing games together.

Still, as a working mom of teens, you can often go days on end without spending a lot of quality time with your kids due to their overloaded schedules—and you miss them! So if you have a choice between seeing your friends, or seeing your kids, the kids should, by default, always come first. So your IRL analog friends might be a bit neglected when you have family, work, or school obligations and you're just too busy to see them. Thank goodness for digital devices that allow us to stay connected even when we aren't IRL often. Digital friends are just as nice, and you can keep up with each other on platforms like Facebook and Instagram! I have to spend a lot of time online for our career, and it's incredibly gratifying to see my growing list of friends online around the world. One of my close friends, Lindsey Stirling, the world's premier hip-hop violinist, is someone that I rarely see, but we totally know what's going on in each other's life since we follow each other online.

One of the very best things about the digital world is how it enables you to find like-minded friends, some close by and some on the other side of the globe. These are people I doubt I will ever meet (although it would be amazing if we did!), but we can become incredibly close and share confidences and ask advice just as we would in person.

Seeing how productive and satisfying these digital global connections have become is an excellent lesson for our kids, too. When Brooklyn went through her first serious breakup, her girlfriends seemed to come out of the woodwork for her. The day they found out what happened, there was a constant stream of girlfriends coming to the house, bringing ice cream and cookies, and notes of support and love. She ended up with this table full of gifts and thoughts from people who wanted her to know they cared about her and who showed up in solidarity and comfort in her time of need. The following week, when her digital friends found out, she received thousands of messages from girls all over the world offering similar words of encouragement, love, and support. Brooklyn was so touched by this kindness, from people she knew she may likely never meet in person. It endeared those online friends to her further.

Tips to finding a good online support group:

- Ask for recommendations from doctors, friends, or other people you trust.
- Look for a narrow objective within the group, for example, moms of autistic children in Dallas.
- Look for a local support group, which can help you connect with a community of people in real life if that's something you're interested in.
- If it's important to you, look for a closed or secret support group, where there is an expectation of confidentiality within the group. Bear in mind, however, that even closed or secret groups are never wholly private, and the Internet is forever. What you thought you posted in confidence might end up being shared anyway.
- Look for a group that has a moderator or facilitator to keep the group clean, without solicitors, etc. You can often find rules or bylaws for how a group is run, and it can be helpful to see if there's anything written down about participants being nonjudgmental, genuinely willing to listen, and ground rules on sharing helpful advice.
- Before settling on a group, check to see whether it's free or there is a membership fee.
- Look for a group that fulfills your cultural, ethical, and religious needs. It's okay to shop around and try out different things to get a clearer sense of what you're looking for, and it's important not to give up! Your tribe is out there, and the Internet makes it easier to find them than ever before.

WHEN FRIENDSHIPS GO WRONG

Just as our children can go through tough times with their friends, sometimes ending a long-standing friendship that we thought would last for years can be hard on us, too. For women who trust and depend on their girlfriends, this can be nearly as painful as a breakup with a long-term romantic partner. Sometimes it's for the best—your interests change, you move away, you change jobs, and so on. Friends can cross behavioral boundaries and make decisions you don't agree with, too, such as drinking too much, making foolhardy life decisions, or having questionable relationships, and it can be hard to be around them when that happens.

Dealing with your people and their personalities is life—and what makes life so interesting. It's good for children to see their parents talking honestly about the ups and downs and pros and cons about their *own* friends—within reason, of course, and in an age-appropriate way. Grown-ups mess up all the time, and this paradoxically can make kids feel better about their own slipups!

I once shared a secret from a friend who had confided in me, and in response, my friend was hurt. She, in turn, reacted very negatively toward me, which left me feeling hurt, too. I talked openly about my poor decision in front of my kids simply because I wanted them to see that I make mistakes, too. That I could also acknowledge my mistakes and take corrective actions. After a while, I was able to see and openly admit my mistake, felt bad, and made amends.

Being able to talk about your situations can also help if your own kids are going through a tough situation or know someone who is—perhaps a friend's parents are separating or getting divorced, or are having a financial downturn, or are dealing with loss. Even young children will appreciate your telling them the truth in an age-appropriate way. If, for example, you have a friend you cherish, but who's always late and drives you crazy with that habit, tell your kids how that makes you feel and why that may seem rude or frustrating. Make sure not to say anything that you wouldn't mind having repeated, and you don't have to have a rant session about your friend, but a simple conversation can help your children understand that all adults have their own quirks and needs, too.

DEALING WITH COMPETITION AND COMPARISONS

I think it's human nature to admire the attributes that aren't naturally yours. I can remember looking at other girls when I was in elementary school, and thinking, *Oh, I wish I was the best dancer.* But I wasn't. I was a late bloomer, and Shaun was, too. We were good at lots of different things and were smart students, but nothing exceptional at any one thing. And now I look at my kids and the things they're doing are things I never would have been able to do at that age. It's so incredible to watch them figure out what their skills are, and see them blossom.

Comparisons are inevitable—it's human nature. You want to make your kids feel empowered by their innate talents, whatever they may be, but it's hard when so many of their peers excel at certain things that might be enviable. And then kids think that their friends' parents are nicer, or homework comes easier, or someone else made the team or the choir and they didn't make the cut.

What I always say to the kids is: The grass may be greener on the other side, but it's just as hard to mow.

Unless you know all the intimate details of what's going on with friends or family, you don't *really* know. It's like seeing all those happy family photos on Instagram and getting a pang that your kids never looked like that, or you can't afford to go to Disney World, or your house is a lot smaller. You're just seeing that one moment in time. It's that Pinterest Phenomenon I mentioned earlier in this book.

Shaun: "I had a friend my age, and we dated in the same circles, hung out with the same crew, got the same grades, spent a lot of time together, came from similar families, and we did pretty much everything the same. I was looking at him on Facebook several months ago and saw that he's been a stay-at-home dad most of his kids' lives, while I've been a dad who's been working and traveling all the time away from home, and I thought to myself, *Oh, my gosh, look at his life, he gets to spend every day with his kids and they'll always remember those moments with him.* But the last time I talked to him, he told me how much he was struggling financially and in his relationship with his spouse…here he is, my friend, in roughly the same time period, looking at me wishing he could have *my* life. Perspective is everything."

While your kids may sometimes have the totally inevitable pangs of jealousy or competition, sharing how *you* feel can be very helpful. Besides, they all know by now that what they see online isn't always real!

COMPARISONS ARE KIND OF POINTLESS!

Friend cliques still exist with adults. Those power plays and shifting dynamics between people who are jealous and/or judgmental of each other can take on a life like the Energizer bunny—they just keep going and going, whether at work, on the playground, at PTA meetings, or even in your own family. It's crazy sometimes how silly and territorial some people can be.

Don't be afraid to be who you are, even if you feel that, at this particular point in your life, you're a bit of an underdog. It's *so* easy to go online and wish you were somebody else. You need to just take care of you and stop with the comparisons.

At our kids' schools, the moms who don't have full-time jobs tend to be the ones who are more involved in school activities. Sometimes I start to question whether I'm present enough, or involved enough. With six children and a demanding career, my time is much more spread out, but if I ever feel like I'm being judged by other moms who think I'm being inattentive, I fall back to the Highlight Reel moments I discussed in Chapter 10. We are making great memories with our children in the way that makes sense for us. I try as hard as I can to make sure I'm always there when the kids are performing. Or if it's a home game, I'm definitely there, but I may not be able to go to all the away games. I still do many of the little things I used to do, like pack them their favorite snacks and leave notes wishing them "Good luck" and saying "I love you."

The topic of comparisons hit home for me not long ago, when I had a conversation with another mom that I knew casually and wanted to get to know a bit better. She told me, "I just don't know how to relate to you—what you do is *so big*! I don't know what we would have to talk about because we don't have anything in common." From my perspective, I felt like our families were incredibly similar and I had been really excited to find somebody with whom I had so much in common. From our kids to our church to where we live, if there had been anyone on this earth who should be able to have things to talk about with me, it would be her! The dividing factor in her mind, which she just could not let go of, was what I do for a career. I thought we would make great friends, but it just isn't happening naturally for me with her, and I need to be okay with that.

Lesson for our kids: *Just because you like someone or want to get to know them doesn't mean they will reciprocate.*

Lesson for me: Since this mom doesn't want to be my friend, I can deal with that! We can wave at each other, be neighborly, and go on our merry way. I don't always have to be first, and can be satisfied with the friends that I do have. I can also still recognize that she's a talented and wonderful wife and mother, even if she doesn't see me as friend material.

There's not a person on earth who isn't looking for connection, to feel seen, to find someone they can share with, relate to, and walk the same path with. Especially once you start having kids and having less time to cultivate relationships outside the home, it can be even harder to be on the same path as someone else. So it can be really discouraging to think you've made a connection, or to see somebody who you line up with on paper, and then to have a real relationship not really spark. When that happens, you have to chalk it up to one of those life experiences, and move on.

DON'T JUDGE OTHER PARENTS TOO HARSHLY IN REAL LIFE OR ONLINE

I have vivid memories of sitting in church and watching my little girls fold their arms reverently as they listened to the speaker—Kamri smiling sweetly at me between coloring pages—and looking at other families with their fidgeting, disruptive children, thinking, *My goodness, what is wrong with you? If you just taught those kids how to behave, you could be like us!*

Then our fourth daughter came along.

It didn't matter if I put her nose in the corner, bribed her, or scolded her—no matter what I did, she climbed on the pews, made too much noise, and even bopped the people sitting in front of us on the head.

When Dax's public behavior was even worse than Rylan's, I had to sit back and laugh about where my life had led me. Rylan was my biological child and Dax was adopted, but they both taught me an incredible lesson: Our children are who they are, not to *spite* us but *despite* us.

You can try to mold them and teach them how to behave, but children each have their own unique personality and needs. Some can sit still; others are born to run. Some are placid and obedient; others never saw a rule they didn't want to break. Some color inside the lines; others will draw all over every page of that coloring book, cut out snowflakes, glue them to the dining room table, add a layer of glitter, and blame it all on the dog.

I'll never again judge parents with loud, unruly, or tantrum-prone children. I simply smile, nod knowingly, and ask if I can help. Sometimes you can't just look at someone and see all that is going on behind the scenes. Often people are struggling in ways that aren't apparent from a quick glance at their exterior person, home life, or business.

When you're a new parent, you're still figuring out your parenting style and how to manage your life with kids. It's awfully easy to get caught up in the whims of the newest parenting trend. Once you get into your groove, and figure out what's best for your particular child, you will likely feel more secure about your parenting style. The biggest challenge once you get into that groove is *not* to assume that what works for you will work for everybody else! I am only offering what rules and structure have worked for us, knowing that these ideas may not work for every family or every child. Take, leave, and adapt what you will. My hope is that you'll be inspired to take a more active role in your children's digital lives.

GETTING GOOD ADVICE CAN BE A LIFESAVER— BUT DON'T LET BAD ADVICE UNDERMINE YOUR PARENTING CONFIDENCE

You know that we don't have all the answers all the time. No one does. Isn't it human nature to seek answers for everything? Don't be afraid to ask others questions about any issue, big or small. Some of the best tips and tricks, life hacks, I have ever received came from moms with much more experience than me. My policy of paying twenty-five cents for every pair of socks the kids match? A great tip from my sister who used it with her own kids. A church friend overheard me talking about how my then-two-year-old Daxton still didn't sleep through the night and told me about over-the-counter dissolvable melatonin tablets. I bought some, and he slept peacefully for the first time in months. A dear friend with much older children gave me a quick cure—an herbal supplement—for mastitis when I was breastfeeding Kamri.

The hardest part is figuring out which of these nuggets will work for you and your family. That's where the "Adapt or Die" strategy you learned about earlier in this book comes in extra-handy!

Because my family is in the public eye, we get a lot of unsolicited advice and comments. While we've had a large number of great recommendations, some of the comments have been less than helpful and, fewer still, can even sometimes be mean, such as "Why would you want to adopt from a race other than your own?" I began to recognize that the opinions of strangers are just that—*opinions.*

No matter who you are, using an online community to make decisions—about parenting or anything else—can be a tricky thing. You have to develop a fairly thick skin so that the unsolicited advice doesn't get overwhelming or painful. That's come only after a *lot* of practice and doing it over and over again. Most people *don't* practice at this, so it can be really hard when your children are small and you're overwhelmed because you're exhausted, and one little innocuous comment leaves you in tears.

Fortunately, I've become better at sifting through unsolicited or unwanted advice, in part because I'm just too busy to have the energy to bother!

HOW TO SIFT THROUGH UNSOLICITED OR UNWANTED ADVICE

Ask the basics. ☺ who, what, when, where, and why.

Who: Who is sending this information to me? Is it someone who *knows* me? Loves me? Cares about me? Or someone who just thinks they know me from momentary snippets online? Is this person someone who cares about my family and my well-being?

What: Is what they are offering as advice relevant? Constructive? Kind? Or mean-spirited?

When: Are they waiting till I am down to throw advice my way? Are they secretly hoping I will fail? Or are they also offering praise and happiness in moments of positivity in my life?

Where: Are they choosing to post this advice in a public forum? Splash it all over Facebook? Or are they personally messaging me and offering sincere thoughts or suggestions?

Why: What is their intention for giving me advice? Are they speaking at me just to hear themselves talk? To try to tell me why my feelings or ideas might be wrong and theirs are correct? To get accolades from other people?

After looking at these questions, it's usually easy to decide which pieces of advice you should listen to and which you should ignore.

One thing I've learned, as I already discussed in Chapter 3, is to keep the sharing to a minimum. You already know that it's okay to have ups and downs with your friends, but keep it private and certainly don't post about it online.

Sometimes being honest online about having a hard time can bring you closer with your digital community. But be thoughtful about what you share, and never post when you're in the real throes of your emotions. Take your time before you put your words out into the world, and never name names no matter how upset or angry you are at the other person. I've seen adults post passive-aggressive comments on different social media platforms just as their kids do when they're hurt, or when they feel slighted. Let me say once more that just because you see something online doesn't mean it's always perfectly truthful!

This is one of the reasons why Shaun and I have always made it a point never to go negative, and our messaging is always going to be positive about our family. That doesn't mean we don't have bad days when we're all yelling at each other! It's just that we choose to focus on the positive.

And remember: Nobody wants to be criticized, but sometimes the advice you don't want to hear is the advice you need to hear the most. When we adopted Paisley, I knew I was going to have to learn how to do her hair. Having her hair look nice would be important as I took her out just like my other daughters, but her hair type is very different from mine, and requires different hair care techniques to maintain its health. I have found much joy in learning about Paisley's hair type and the fun new hairstyles that test my skills. Culturally her hair care is important and I didn't want other moms thinking I couldn't or wouldn't take care of it because I was Caucasian. Occasionally, in comments, I'll receive negative feedback about her hair, or questions asking what types of products I am using for her. I often answer and explain that I'm still learning, and would love their well-meaning input.

Sometimes when people can see I'm trying my best and willing to accept advice, they quickly switch gears and begin a very friendly dialogue with me. I've received some of the best tips on products to use on natural hair when I have opened up and been honest about the fact that I am still learning. Even though their initial comments might be interpreted as hurtful, I try to see through them for the advice I desperately need without getting my feelings hurt.

YOUR EXTENDED FAMILY

There is an element of truth to the old adage that you can't choose your family but you can choose your friends. We did choose the two children we adopted, and love them unconditionally as much as our biological children. We have tons of extended family, with countless cousins on both sides, and every time we move to a new location, we joke that we collect family wherever we go. My kids are very fortunate to have several people they think are aunts, uncles, and grandparents who are not biologically related to any of us, but they're enough of a part of our lives that we all act like they are family. We *choose* to be family. Your family is who you love, and the more people who love your children, the better off they will be.

We've had family that has been here to help at the drop of a hat when we needed them. I've also had friends that have been there when family couldn't, after I delivered a baby, for instance. We've learned some of our best family traditions from our friends, while I still recite a million phrases to my children that my mom said to me growing up. I love that our family dynamic is a beautiful mixture of people and relationships all woven together, through love and not just blood.

USING DIGITAL COMMUNICATION TO STAY IN TOUCH

We have friends whose parents are staunchly analog, and just can't seem to grasp the workings (and wonders) of digital communication. We're lucky that our kids' grandparents do amazingly well with technology. They're not always super-savvy, but they all have laptops and smartphones, and regularly use Facebook and Instagram.

This makes staying in touch so much better, a thousand times over! My parents follow my kids' accounts, and when my mom watches all of their videos, she feels connected to them even though we don't live physically close. What's also great is how easy it is for them to connect with the kids on their own devices instead of needing to route any messages or calls through me or Shaun.

Digital communication also makes it a lot easier to filter out what and how much you want to share with your family. One of our youth leaders at church asked my advice about getting to know the twins better, without my girls thinking she was being too invasive. I told her simply to follow them online. Following the girls on their social platforms gives that church leader a general overview of their likes and interests, the activities they are involved in, which then allows her to ask specific questions about their lives in order to form a deeper and more meaningful relationship. This is particularly helpful for family members who want you to know they're interested in what's going on in your lives, even if they don't visit often or have a lot of free time to talk or write.

If nothing else, I love social media and digital communication for the fun they bring into our family. I love seeing my girls comment and leave positive thoughts on each other's posts. I also love that we have a family text tree where we regularly share photos, funny jokes, new trends, or ask questions. Our text tree brings out the funny side in all of us...especially when Shaun uses the wrong emojis, or texts us all a lame Dad joke, which is his specialty.

It's fun to see the girls grow and mature in their style, their humor, and their knowledge on their own. They are developing their own relationships with us on their own terms, instead of us having only a stiff "Because I said so" kind of parent-child relationship. Yes, we are still parents, not their best friends, but as our teens grow up and show us how trustworthy they are, and that they desire to succeed in life, they receive more freedom in our system and our relationships grow stronger.

Chapter 13

The Digital Teeter-Totter

Brooklyn: "We have been spoon-fed a steady diet of technology, iPhones, TV shows, apps, instant messaging, and video games since our birth. It's all we know, and we have learned to fully integrate and revolve our lives around it. Our parents make up the generation that introduced us to this digital era, but sometimes struggle at needing to learn how to be self sufficient in this world themselves. I'm not sure as to why parents are exasperated when their children are so connected with technology!"

THE TODDLER TRUTH

The first time you try anything new—as you found out when you tried to use Snapchat for the first time—you're not going to be comfortable doing it, because you're not good at it yet. Why would you expect to be?

That's the Toddler Truth. Toddlers are so busy learning everything (and getting their delicious little hands *into* everything!) that when they first start to walk, they fall down fifty-six times a day, pick themselves right back up, and go back to their exploration. (And it's rare for them to cry unless you go running over to them and make a fuss.)

They have no fear of failure because they don't expect to be proficient at something that they're learning. It's always about moving forward and learning as much as they can.

The first time you drive a car, you're not going to be good at it. It's going to be terrifying; you'll be nervous and scared and will probably cry. I did, and our girls did! Especially the first time they pulled out wrong into traffic and got an angry honk. "I don't want to drive anymore!" they cried. "We're never doing this again!" Well, if you give in to their fears, then they will never do it again, so you know that they have to get back behind the wheel the next time and keep going. Eventually, they're totally fine, and can't believe they ever worried about driving.

Baby steps all the way. When Brooklyn and Bailey were getting ready to go on tour with a live set in 2017, I had them rehearse their choreography here in town first, to get their learning curve done in private rather than in front of twenty people in a studio in Los Angeles. I knew that would make them even more comfortable when the time would come for them to go onstage in front of an audience.

For me, I'm not a comfortable ad-lib speaker, believe it or not. Some people can just walk onstage and talk for thirty minutes and never have a note in front of them—that would give me heart palpitations! But I know that I can speak comfortably if I have my notes at the ready. In fact, when we started making our videos, I extremely disliked being in front of the camera. I was so nervous and sweaty the first few times we gave interviews to the press, and I still don't like walking the red carpet, but my girls are champs at it. We all just have different comfort levels.

You want to take a lesson from the Toddler Truth and apply it to your entire life. Get out and explore. Sure, you'll fall, but you'll pick yourself right back up. Push yourself out of your analog comfort zone and become the digitally savvy parent you know you can be. Your kids need to see you doing it—even if you get the eye rolls when you start following them on Instagram! They need to see you trying, and maybe failing at first, but that's okay. You know that, with perseverance, you'll succeed.

It's not just about mastering technology, but about you instilling a firm sense of self-confidence in your accomplishments, no matter how small. This self-confidence will come from knowing that you are doing your best for your children and preparing not just them but possible future generations. Remember, we are the parents that are setting new rules and new parenting for everyone as this digital landscape is like the Wild, Wild West of old.

Digital self-confidence comes with diligence in exercising your digital muscles over and over each day. On some days, it's hard to get motivated, but on others, it will be easy. There will be days of pulling your hair out and being so frustrated with your children, their choices, or the digital space in general. But as you build that confidence through diligence and practice, you will be able to step back, look at where you started, and also teach your children to respect and be proud of their own accomplishments. Have you ever seen the before-and-after photos from friends that start going to the gym? If you are around them every day for six months, you might not notice all the small changes in their bodies and health. But then when you see their before-and-after photos, suddenly it's so obvious how much work they have been putting in at the gym and how it's paying off on their bodies, their confidence, and their health.

Digital diligence is much the same way. Day to day you may not notice all the changes and effects of minor choices and small lessons. But six months later you will look back on all you have learned, all the conversations you have had with your children, and all the lessons you have started to instill in them, and suddenly you will get your own before-and-after images of your digital exercises and all their payoff.

Most important, teaching your children self-respect is actually what will protect them from the hazards of social media and the digital world. As our kids have said, when you know that you're a good person and what you do is good, then it doesn't matter what other people say or do. This is the crucial emotional tool that will cover your children in digital Teflon, so that any potential negativity and snarky comments will slide right off them and never stick.

The more analog moments your children have, the more they will be able to build up the thicker skin for not just when those digital moments are hurtful, but when they tackle whatever life is going to throw at them. Yes, they will survive if their cell phone is turned off for a few minutes when you sit down to talk to them about what's going on in their world!

BELIEVING IN YOURSELF TEACHES YOUR CHILDREN HOW TO BELIEVE IN THEMSELVES

We are a faith-driven family, and contributing to our community is incredibly important to us. Giving back to those in need is one of the best ways to take children offline and help them become confident and loving citizens of the world.

Shaun: "Our faith has created a very strong foundation for who we are as people, how we raise our kids, and how we run our business. When you are part of a faith community, you have something in common with everybody else who is worshiping with you. You're all in the same room with the same purpose—to deepen your faith. We strive to go to church every Sunday, and mid-week Bible class starts when the kids are fourteen. They go before school starts every day, and like all teenagers, they may grumble about having to get up early, but they still never miss a class unless they're sick or out of town. It's just part of who they are, and I know they relish the time to focus their days on bigger things before heading off into the world. It also gives them a circle of friends from all over the area, not just from their school, which is always a good thing.

"What our children have learned is that when you start your day off by centering your thoughts on matters of the soul, even if only for a few minutes, it tends to let your day run a little bit better. You're bringing yourself peace and comfort—and we can all use more of that!

"But you don't have to believe in organized religion to have faith. Anyone can develop their own system of spiritual beliefs to guide them. I think it's really important to have something outside that's bigger than you, especially in the new digital age when real-life connections will still be the most important things you will ever have in your life.

"I also believe that if you remove the notion of God from faith, what you still have is hope. Whether by believing in God's goodness and guidance to improve your life and the life of your family, or whether by hoping that acting with goodness will bring goodness to you, the goal is still the same in all aspects of life. Faith and hope both accomplish the same thing—a desire for a better outcome for you and all your loved ones."

USING APPS TO STAY GROUNDED

One of the most wonderful categories of apps is the one for guided meditations, motivational or scripture sayings, and prayers. There are thousands to choose from, and they make it incredibly easy to spend as little as a minute or two, or much longer if you have the time, to focus yourself, clear your mind, help you set your intentions for the day, and find a moment to be grateful and centered. These apps are a perfect example of using digital technology to give yourself an analog experience. They're also great for guiding you through controlled breathing, or a moment to reflect on a profound verse or statement, which can help calm you and your children instantly when they're feeling particularly stressed.

TEACHING YOUR CHILDREN TO THINK OUTSIDE OF THEMSELVES

Our church, the Church of Jesus Christ of Latter-day Saints, like all houses of worship, is about much more than mere tenets of our faith. It's about developing leadership skills. It's about learning patience and respect for others. It's about philanthropy. It's about becoming part of a community larger than the one you live in.

What it also does is reinforce how we teach our children about believing in *themselves*. In their basic goodness, in their potential, and in their loving and generous spirit.

We've noticed how our church has become more active on social media to make a difference. In fact, they created a social media campaign just for its members, centered around the notion that one way to combat so much of the negativity we see all around us is with a targeted campaign. The message was: When you do something good or see someone do something good, share it and use the hashtag #sharegoodness. Since we're social media influencers, this was an ideal way for us to get the word out. We saw how well this worked after Hurricane Harvey, when we shared information about how to volunteer at a local distribution center to sort through the donations.

What we wanted to do was inspire our viewers and fans to do the same in their own community.

It doesn't matter what your religion is. I don't care what your beliefs, color, or sexuality with which you identify are—simply do good and be nice to people. It's not that hard!

Volunteering is an important part of our lives. Last year, for example, we gave service as a family to a neighbor. Their house had been struck by lightning, and caught fire. We organized a group of nearly two dozen people who went to the house to help with the cleanup, as there had been a lot of smoke and water damage on all the floors, from the top down into the basement. It was hard and dirty work on a day when the temperature was in the triple digits, but it had an amazing payoff. Not only were our kids happy to help out and see how much they accomplished after what could have been an even worse disaster, but the homeowner turned that lemon situation into lemonade by doing the long-overdue clean-out that she'd been putting off. She had a big pile of the vintage board games—even the version of Monopoly that Shaun and I had grown up with—and she told the girls to take whatever they wanted as a thank-you. They were thrilled, and started playing them when they arrived home.

"Wow, Mom," they said, "this old Monopoly board is so much better than playing on an app!" Score for the analog team!

BROOKLYN, ON VOLUNTEERING

When you are blessed with many great things in life, I believe it is your responsibility to turn around and bless others that are less fortunate, whether it be with your time, talent, or money. In the summer of 2016, Bailey and I were able to participate in my favorite service project in Peru, building a school there for a community in need. Through this experience we were able to see how these people who had very little were able to be happy and grateful for every small and simple thing they were given in life. It was truly inspiring to see, and the experience shed a new light on the importance of service, and the blessings that are given to both those providing and those receiving.

LIVE IN THE PRESENT. THE FUTURE WILL BE HERE BEFORE YOU KNOW IT!

We live in a competitive society. Parents regularly go through a familiar litany—"Are the schools in my area good enough that my kids can go to a good college, and find the perfect partner, and get married and have their own family?"—until they remember that their kids are only five and have just started kindergarten! What are we doing?

I constantly have to remind myself to stop living for the future. My kids are growing up so quickly. I already can't believe that our twins are out of the house, off on their own adventures at college. How can that be? Wasn't it just yesterday that they were tiny little girls sitting in the bathroom while I decided what hairstyle would look best that morning?

Of course, you need to think about the future, but you also have to keep your eyes on the prizes sitting in the room with you, scrolling through the texts on their phones, right this very minute. Even if you've all had the worst day ever, it is *your* day and *your* family, and love will pull you through.

Finding the ideal mix of analog and digital is what will pull *you* through the tough job of being a parent. We're living through an amazing moment in history, akin to the invention of the printing press, the electric lightbulb, or the television. The digital revolution has totally changed how we live. We're on the cusp of even more amazing changes.

Still, this also makes me worry that our senses are losing out—especially when we stop using our voices to talk on the phone and text instead, and stop using our fingers to touch people while we keep on touching electronic screens. Real life is all about touch. You're never going to get that typing on a keyboard or swiping on a screen, and as amazing as virtual reality can be, even if you put on state-of-the-art techno gloves to simulate pressure, it will never be the actual feel of the human touch.

Another digital revolution looming on the horizon is AI (artificial intelligence). Not that long ago, I saw a viral video with robot dogs who'd figured out how to open a door. It was equally riveting and kind of terrifying! Not only that, but AI has already invaded all your digital devices by predicting what you want to see and hear and shop for with the newest forms of technology—not only can advertisers access your surfing history to deliver targeted ads, but your computer or phone may also be potentially listening in on your conversations (especially if you have Alexa, Google, or use Facebook on your phone), and then indexing keywords on your device from what *you* said that can then be accessed by ad servers to place specific ads on the sites you visit, whether you want to see them or not.

This means you need to pay attention to what you're talking about with your kids if your devices are turned on and potentially listening! You'll start to notice that things you *never* searched for on your phone or computer have suddenly appeared in the form of ads only because you talked about them in an innocuous conversation! (If you've seen the movie *2001*, this might remind you of the computer HAL running amok.) Both Facebook and Instagram have the ability to do this using your phone. We've tested this time and time again to know it isn't coincidence. It's *crazy*!

And although the convenience and pleasure of being able to stream thousands of different movies and TV shows on your computer or large-screen TV is truly a marvel, watching them at home will never replicate the experience of seeing a movie in a large, darkened theater, on an enormous screen, with people surrounding you and jumping out of their seats when the bad guy opens the door to the basement, or when the good guy finally gets to kiss the girl!

This kind of communal pleasure is something we also see when we go to meet-ups with our fans and viewers, especially for the girls. The people who come from all over the world to meet Brooklyn and Bailey have never met each other, but they have so much in common, and they've followed each other on social media, so the meeting instantly feels comfortable and familiar. I never get tired of watching this happen. Sometimes I talk to the fans waiting in line, and I ask them how they heard about the girls, and they'll say, "Oh, I first saw them when I was four and my mom did my hair before school, too." They've all become part of the same tribe—and during these meet-ups, the digital world becomes real when they actually get to hug the girls. It's incredibly gratifying and thrilling for everyone.

At the end of the day, we all have the same needs. The need to be loved, the need to have purpose, the need to be productive, and the need to nourish ourselves. Those are analog needs.

As young parents in this interesting period of time, we had the unique opportunity of growing up at the tail end of analog and watching the birth of the Digital Native Generation, as we explained earlier in this book. This allowed us the one singularly unique chance to take and embrace the best of both worlds. We can appreciate the digital because we so clearly remember the past of analog when things were slower and sometimes cumbersome. But it also makes us appreciate the analog moments that can sometimes be more mean-ingful, like face-to-face interaction and communication.

But like anything in life, digital can be a double-edged sword…a delicate balancing act of utilizing digital and taking advantage of the ease and speed of new technology while managing to keep your kids grounded with a firm foundation of analog moments.

I call it the digital teeter-totter.

Imagine a teeter-totter with digital on one end and analog on the other. If you stack too many digital moments or experiences on one end, the teeter-totter tips and everything on that end crashes to the ground. But stack too many experiences and moments on the analog side of the seat, and you're in jeopardy of analog crashing down.

One of the goals of this book as it relates to parenting in this age is to help us all figure out that perfect balance. That magical moment where the analog and the digital perfectly align and the teeter-totter balances into a perfect straight line in harmony on both sides.

In an ever-developing world, where technology seemingly dupli-cates at a faster rate than it ever has, one thing will never change—the link between a parent and a child, and the love a family has for each other.

For all the tips, tricks, rules, systems, and experiences that I shared in this book, this is what I hope you'll take away from it. We are the chosen generation, given the important responsibility to connect two completely different worlds. *We are the bridge!* As such, we decide what simple and beautiful analog moments to keep, as well as what new, exciting, and advanced technologies we allow our children to experience. We become the standard bearers for our children, who will then use our baseline tech-savvy parenting examples with their own children. But it starts with us. We'll have only one chance to raise these children, to set these standards, and it's critical that we rise to the occasion. We can no longer afford, for the sake of our kids, to sit idly by watching as technology transforms our children without also interjecting ourselves into the same transformations. If we can do this in an effective manner, we will arm our children with the knowledge they need to prepare future generations for continued technological advances while still maintaining the best balance from both analog and digital worlds.

Acknowledgments

This book would have been impossible to write without the help of so many people. I'll never adequately thank or recognize everyone that played a part in me bringing this to reality.

To Shaun: My partner in life, in love, in work, and in play. You journeyed through these experiences right alongside me. You believed in my dreams, my hobbies, and my sometimes crazy ideas before anybody else. I would not be who I am and where I am without you. I love you!

To Brooklyn, Bailey, Kamri, Rylan, Daxton, and Paisley: You were not only my amazing children, but effectively my study subjects throughout this process! Thank you for your helpful insights, always having honest conversations with me, and being patient while I tried to figure out parenting, technology, YouTube, and everything else. Forgive me for the mistakes I've made along the way. Know that I have always loved you and always will.

To my parents: You started the process of teaching me how to parent, and I honor and thank you for the wonderful childhood I enjoyed. I cherish my memories of laughter and camping and a million other happy moments centered around you two.

To Amy Neben: You're the best manager we could have asked for. You've encouraged and provided me ways to accomplish more than I thought I was capable of. We could not do this without you.

To Karen Moline: Thank you for the endless hours of work on this book. Your energy reading, re-reading, editing, and providing

...sightful feedback helped to give this book its wings. Here's to life, family, and Texas Twinkies! ☺

To Ellie Altshuler, Steve Troha, Sana Sherali, Leah Miller, and my extended Hachette team...Don't think just because you work in the shadows on this book that I don't know how much you do for me and making my *Viral Parenting* book come true. Thanks to you all!

About the Author

Mindy McKnight launched the CuteGirlsHairstyles.com website in late 2008 and the subsequent CuteGirlsHairstyles YouTube channel in early 2009. While Mindy's hairstyle tutorials began as a hobby, they have paved the way to a large family social media empire including over 23 million followers across all social platforms, six successful YouTube channels, and several highly successful off-platform businesses. The video content created has now been viewed more than 2 billion times worldwide. Mindy has been ranked as one of the Top 25 Women on YouTube, with over 5.6 million subscribers, generating 10 million monthly views. The family has received local, national, and global attention through various media outlets including ABC-News' *20/20*, *Good Morning America*, *TODAY*, *Anderson LIVE*, *Katie*, and *The View*.